M000233734

Valleys
OF THE
Shadow

by
Sheila Robertson

as told by
Janice Hampton Quick

FAIRHAVEN MEDIA

Valleys of the Shadow
Copyright 2017© by Sheila Robertson

This title is also available as a Fairhaven Media ebook.
Visit www.amazon.com.

All photos provided by the family unless otherwise noted.

All rights reserved. No part of this publication may be reproduced, stored in a retrieval system, or transmitted in any form or by any means—electronic, mechanical, photo-copy, recording, or any other—except for brief quotations in printed reviews, without the prior permission of the publisher.

Cover design: Izzit Graphics *www.izzitgraphics.com*
Interior design: Sheila Robertson

Printed in the United States of America

ISBN: 978-0-9987480-9-2
Domestic Violence, Domestic Abuse, Family Matters

Janice's Dedication

Dedicated to my mama and daddy,
Wilma and Joe Hampton,
and my sister, Kay Cunningham
I would never have made it without you.
I love you.

Sheila's Dedication

Dedicated to Janice, Joey, Jason and Julie
What you have suffered through and
won victory over,
is the stuff from which heroes are made.
Thank you and our Lord Jesus Christ
for allowing me to share your story.

Acknowledgements

I would like to thank a few people for their friendship and support: my Pastor, Jack Hice, who has walked with me through many hard days; my lifelong friend, Maxine; and the nurses, CNA's, staff and my nurse practitioner Katie Gilliland at the facility where I live. I would also like to mention my beautiful nieces, Kim and Jada, and my wonderful son-in-law and daughter-in-law. I'm so happy that we are family.

The last person that I would like to acknowledge is Sheila. Thank you for your hard work and patience as we worked our way through the pain.

Janice

I would like to thank the many people that helped me during the process of writing this book. Of course, the biggest help that I had was from my savior Jesus Christ. Without His help I wouldn't have made my way through the pain that I was trying to express. Thank you to my husband who read and re-read every page of the book, and offered valuable suggestions and editing. Thank you to my mama who listened to my heartache during the process with a loving ear. Thank you to the ladies that helped edit the manuscript: Marleeta Yardumian, Patti Towry, Terri Totty, Debbie Brooks, Emily Yardumian, and Hazel Liner.

Thank you to all the people that shared their memories: Earla and Randy Alexander, Bonnie Philpott, Pastor Donald Gregory, Kathleen Lawson, Maxine Dean, and Cindy Smith.

I would also like to honor Diane Sawyer, who has gone home to be with the Lord, for years ago recording some of the details of Janice's story that might have been lost to memory by now.

If Janice, Joey, Jason, and Julie had not opened up their hearts to me, shared their pain, their disappointments, their hurts, and their struggles, then none of this would have been possible. Thank you for allowing me to be part of your ongoing story. I love you all.

Sheila

Panic was rising in her throat and the smell of gunpowder was burning her nostrils. Doors opening and closing. Burst of light. Distant shouts. Blinding pain flashing through her head. The child next to her screaming. She reached to comfort the child and her arms fell limp. Waves of terror rolled over her as she realized that she couldn't move, but the fear was swimming upstream against the inner pain that threatened to drown her. *Somebody help me...*

Chapter 1

How did it ever come to this? Janice lay motionless in the emergency room of Baptist Hospital in Nashville, Tennessee. Doctors and nurses scurried around trying to assess the damage done to her and her mother Wilma. Only her dad was there with them. Although he was suffering from pneumonia, he insisted on riding in the front of the ambulance. No one else from the family had made it to the hospital yet. The 70-mile trip had been chaotic. Janice, Wilma, two nurses, and a paramedic were all crammed into the back of an ambulance. Janice tried to turn her head to see her mother but she couldn't. Mercifully, Wilma was spared the trauma of the ambulance ride; she was unconscious.

Even though she was unconscious, every so often she would call out, "Baby?"

"Tell her you are here," the paramedic said to Janice. "Let her hear you."

"I'm here, Mama. I'm alive," Janice said.

If the ambulance ride was chaotic, the emergency room was pandemonium: machines beeping, buzzers going off, people running past her. The confusion matched her mood. Processing what had just happened to them was impossible. How do you handle the idea that your life has just been altered forever? Maybe even taken from you completely?

A thousand things ran through her mind. If only I had not done this. If only I had done that. Tormenting thoughts chasing themselves around in endless circles. Would she live through the night? Would her mother? Were her children all right? Who was helping them through this nightmare?

Her thoughts were interrupted as one of the emergency room doctors and the neurosurgeon approached her. "Can you tell me what happened?" asked the emergency room doctor.

"Yes. My mother was shot twice and I was hit in the head with the gun and shot once," Janice answered, surprisingly lucid.

"Let me check your head," the neurosurgeon said as he turned Janice's head to the side. "Mrs. Quick, you have a bullet lodged in your head. You weren't hit with the gun. You were shot in the head."

"What?! I was shot in the head?" she asked.

"Yes ma'am. You were also shot in the spine. Right now you are paralyzed, but we won't know the extent of your injuries until we can operate. You are not stable enough for surgery, so we are going to put you in the intensive care unit until it is safe to operate. I know this seems impossible, but try to rest."

Yeah, that's impossible.

"Where's my mother?" she asked the emergency

room doctor as he started to walk away.

"They've already taken her to surgery. She's in pretty bad shape, but she's holding her own. We will let you know something as soon as we get word."

Janice lay quietly as they wheeled her to the intensive care unit. She was at least temporarily paralyzed, and her mother was undergoing what would be a six-hour surgery to save her life. *Yea, though I walk through the valley of the shadow of death...* Janice knew that many times in the past twelve years that she had walked through countless valleys, and several times she came close to the shadow of death. However, this was far beyond anything she had ever imagined or expected. This nightmare wasn't over; it was just the beginning of a new chapter.

Chapter 2

Storm Warnings

The strawberry blonde sophomore sat in the stands at the football game that Friday night with her friends, Karen and Nancy. The game was at a standstill to remove an injured player from the field. The center had been hit hard on the last play and was being carried off.

"That was W.J. Quick that just got hurt!" Karen said.

"Oh no! Do you think he's okay?" Janice answered, a hint of panic in her voice.

"Yeah, he'll be okay. You're just scared you won't get to go on your double date tomorrow night," Nancy laughed at her.

"No, that's not it. I'm seriously worried that he's hurt...but....I don't want to miss my date with him. I can't believe I'm going out with a senior and the starting center!" Janice was trying to hide her excitement but Karen and Nancy weren't fooled. They knew their friend all too well.

W.J. ran back onto the field and finished the game without any further problems. The next night, Jerry, Jane, and W.J. went to Janice's house to hang out and listen to records. Later, they went riding around. It was October 15, 1960, two weeks away from her 15th birthday, and Janice Hampton was going on her first official date with W.J. Quick, the good-looking senior football player. Her starry eyed crush was understandable. He was handsome, well-liked and did well academically. He was a real trophy, especially for a sophomore, and all her friends envied her.

However, W.J. wasn't just two years ahead of her in school. He had been raised in Alabama and wasn't allowed to start school until he turned seven years old. Due to family circumstances and moving out of state, he was two grades behind his age group; therefore, he was five years older than her. He had already turned twenty by the time they had their first date.

After their first date, they talked a lot in school the following week and Janice couldn't wait until the next weekend, when there would be a Friday night football game and another date with W.J.

Friday nights in Tullahoma were like Friday nights in hundreds of other small towns in Tennessee. The high school football game was the place to be, the social highlight of the week. After the game, Janice was going with W.J. and his friends to a favorite hangout. It was a large field on the edge of town. W.J. had told her how they would sit on the hoods of their cars and talk for hours. Sometimes they would turn on a car radio and start dancing.

When W.J. finished all the post game requirements, they jumped in his white Volkswagen Bug and headed to the field.

"You sure looked good out on the field tonight," Janice complimented him.

"Not half as good as that cute blonde I saw in the stands," W.J. answered. "I wonder if she would go out with me," he laughed, teasing her.

Janice poked at him. He was in a great mood and she was excited about going to the 'field'. She had heard kids at school talking about it, but never thought she would be cool enough to go. Now, here she was, on her way to spend time with the starting center of the football team and all his upperclassman friends. The thought of the evening made her feel very grown-up.

Many of his friends were already there when they pulled into the field. They stood around talking for a while. The guys, mostly football players, were busy rehashing every play of the game while the girls were busy talking about the guys.

"Janice, it's 10:45," W.J. interrupted the girls discussion of the latest hair styles. "I don't want to be late getting you home." It seemed that time went faster on Friday nights than any other time during the week.

As Janice walked hand in hand with W.J. back to his car, she heard one of the girls remark on how lucky she was to have him for a boyfriend. She smiled to herself. She knew how lucky she was and she liked the feeling of the older girls envying her. She knew all her friends envied her too, that is, everybody except her sister Kay who despised W.J. for some unknown reason.

"Do you think your mother would mind if I came in

Janice Hampton High School Junior Year 1961/1962

W.J Quick High School Junior Year 1959/1960

for a little while?" he asked her as they pulled into her parent's driveway.

"No, she won't mind. She said we could sit in the living room and watch television after my curfew. I think she might even let you stay until midnight," Janice said.

Kay was still watching television when they entered the living room.

"What's he doing here?" she asked.

"Kay, it's your bedtime. Get ready for bed," their mother Wilma told her.

Kay reluctantly got up and started toward her bedroom.

Janice and W.J. enjoyed sitting close to each other on the couch for as long as her mother would allow. After Wilma told W.J. that it was time to leave, she and Janice sat for another hour or so talking. Wilma was particularly protective and she wanted to be the perfect mother for her daughters. Her own mother had died when she was just 11 years old, so she missed out on sharing her teenage life with a mother. Being involved in Janice and Kay's lives was a priority for her.

The next morning, Janice and Kay helped their mother clean the house. It was a Saturday morning chore and there was just no getting out of it. Wilma was an exceptional housekeeper and would not stand for her house to get messy. She knew it was good training for her daughters to get into the habit of keeping a clean house.

"Is W.J. coming over here again today?" Kay asked, disgusted at the thought.

"Kay! Why do you not like W.J.?" Wilma asked,

shocked at her daughter's attitude toward him.

"I just don't like him. He's too possessive! He's always walking with her at school and watching her every move," she exclaimed. Kay had never had a problem speaking her mind. She didn't like him, and she didn't care who knew it.

Janice and Kay were more like twins than sisters. They were born one year and one day apart. Janice was the oldest and she thought that maybe Kay was feeling a little left out since she had started dating. W.J. did take a lot of her focus and attention, but that was all part of growing up. She hoped that Kay's attitude would change when she was old enough to date.

"Kay, you just simmer down! W.J. is a nice young man. He's coming over here today to help me in the flower garden so you be nice to him. And stop picking on your sister," Wilma scolded her.

"I'll be nice to him, but I'm never gonna like him," Kay said as she stomped out of the kitchen to go clean somewhere else in the house.

"Janice, don't you be upset about Kay. You know that your daddy and I like W.J. and we don't mind him coming by on Saturdays. Kay will warm up to him in time. Your dad said that he could come on a Sunday afternoon drive with us tomorrow if he wants to. Why don't you ask him when he's over here?" Janice could always count on her parents to support her.

W.J. endeared himself to Janice's parents. Wilma and Joe saw him many times that first month that they dated. He came over, mowed their lawn without being asked, and brought fertilizer from the farm for Wilma's flowers. They all loved this nice, young man that was so kind, considerate, and good to their daughter, everyone, that is, except Kay. She continued to dislike W.J.

The fall school semester rushed by in a blur. Although Janice's social schedule was full with Library Club, Future Homemakers of America, Pep Club, Drama Club, and, of course, W.J., she never struggled with her school work. She always made all A's and B's, but she had one little habit she couldn't break. She bit her nails.

"Janice, you really need to stop biting your nails," W.J. told her.

"I know, but it's hard," she answered.

She decided that she would work hard to grow her nails out and stop biting them. For a month she did great and the results were beautiful. She trimmed and fixed her nails, polishing them a pretty color before W.J. picked her up for a date. As they sat in the driveway at the end of the evening, she was proudly showing him her nails.

"They're too long," he said, never complimenting her on the effort, "you need to cut them."

She continued to stare at her nails. She didn't want to cut them. It took a long time and a lot of effort to get them that long. She looked up at him not believing that he could ask her to do that.

"Don't you smirk at me like that!" he said.

Janice had no idea that she had smirked at all. Confused, she looked back down at her nails and up at him again.

"I told you not to smirk at me like that," he said as

he violently slapped her.

She sat there in shock. Her head was ringing, her face was stinging and her heart was breaking. *What had brought that on?*

She looked back up at W.J. as he started hitting his head on the steering wheel.

"Oh, Janice! I'm so sorry. Please forgive me. I don't know why I did that. I promise I'll never do anything like that again. Are you okay?" He apologized as he beat his head repeatedly against the steering wheel.

"Yes...I think I'm okay," she said with her face still stinging.

She got out of the car and went in the house. Her parents were watching television as she walked into the living room.

"What's wrong Janice?" her dad asked.

"W.J. just hit me," she said still in shock.

"He hit you?!" Wilma asked.

"Yes, he hit me and then he started hitting his head on the steering wheel as he apologized to me," she explained.

Joe was furious. "He is not welcome in our house anymore," he said.

"And I don't think you need to see him anymore," Wilma added.

"That sounds like a good idea," Janice agreed as she walked down the hall to her bedroom.

The next morning, Janice and Kay were getting ready for school. They shared a bathroom and mornings were hectic as they both tried to do their hair and makeup. Listening to the radio always seemed to calm them, but it wasn't helping Janice this morning. She had decided to tell Kay what had happened the night before, even though she knew what Kay's reaction would be.

"Kay, I wanted to tell you something but please don't get upset. Last night W.J. slapped me," Janice explained.

"He did WHAT?!" she all but shouted. "Why that dirty, no good bum. Did you tell Mama and Daddy?"

"Yes, I did and they said he was no longer welcome in our house."

"Good! I hope I see him at school today. I'll give him a piece of my mind. How dare he hit you! He better never do it again," she said.

"Calm down, Kay. He won't have the opportunity to hit me again, because Mama said that I shouldn't see him anymore, and I agree," Janice told her.

The phone in their room rang. Janice and Kay were fortunate enough to have their own phone line. Their uncle had lived with them for a while after his divorce and he had a second phone installed in Wilma and Joe's house. After he moved out on his own, he left the phone for his nieces and continued to pay the bill. Janice answered and it was W.J..

"Can I come over?" W.J. asked.

"No, you can't come over. My parents said you are not welcome in their house anymore after hitting me last night. I'm getting ready for school so don't come over," Janice told him.

He hung up. She heard something and looked up.

W.J. was walking down the hallway toward her bedroom. He had slipped into the other end of the house and called Janice and Kay's phone from their parents' phone in the living room.

When Kay heard W.J.'s voice, she ran out of the bathroom in a rage, "You better get out of this house before I call the police. You can't see my sister anymore. You good for nothing piece of trash! Don't you ever touch her again!" He turned around and left.

Later that week, W.J. approached Wilma and Joe and apologized to them for hitting their daughter. He promised them that nothing like that would ever happen again.

Despite her parents continued concerns, Janice started dating W.J. again. He had shown no other signs of abusiveness and she began to think that the one incident might have been just a fluke.

Not long after that, at school one day, W.J. ran up to Janice at her locker.

"Why are you grinning from ear to ear?" she asked. She could tell by his excitement that he had something to tell her.

"I made the All Mid-State football roster! And I also made honorable mention for All-State," he all but shouted.

"W.J., that's great!" she exclaimed, "I'm so proud of you. What a great honor! All Mid-State! But why didn't they pick you for All-State? You're better than any other center that I've seen. You deserve better than honorable mention."

During this discussion, John, who had been friends with Janice since elementary school, walked by.

"Hi Janice," John innocently said.

"Hi John," she answered without thinking or even looking up.

"Hi John?" Turning to Janice, W.J. angrily asked, "What are you doing flirting with other guys?"

"W.J., I wasn't flirting. That was John. We've known each other since first grade. He's just an old friend. I wouldn't dream of flirting with him," Janice answered, surprised at his jealousy.

He grabbed her and slammed her against the locker. Other students standing nearby watched in horror.

"Don't you ever flirt with another guy," he growled at her.

He released her and walked off. Janice stood there shaking. Maybe the other incident wasn't just a fluke after all, however, they still continued to see each other.

*****

In May 1961, W.J. graduated from high school and went to work full time for a local moving and storage company. He had worked part time through high school for the same business. However, before Christmas that year, he changed jobs. He was now working for a furniture company.

Janice realized that Kay had been right. W.J. was too possessive and she was tired of it. She decided to break up with him. He was wonderful most of the time, but on top of the possessiveness, there was something just under the surface that wasn't pretty. She told him they were through and he asked if she would go for a ride with him to talk things over. She agreed to discuss the breakup, so he picked her up and started driving toward Lynchburg.

He kept begging her not to break up, but she stood firm that it was over. W.J. started getting agitated.

"W.J., take me home please," Janice said.

He turned the car around and started back. By then, his agitation had grown to full-fledged anger.

"I'm going to drive this car right off a cliff and kill both of us!" he threatened.

Although these kind of remarks scared Janice, she simply felt he was being dramatic.

"Fine! I won't break up with you, just take me home," she gave in.

Instead of breaking up after he returned her to her home, Janice stayed with him. She started her junior year in high school, but she continued to speak to her friends that were guys, despite W.J.'s warnings. Janice was determined not to snub her friends just to satisfy his insecurities.

Christmas 1961 was approaching and W.J. was working on a special surprise for Janice. He was building her a hope chest, which was a small chest that young girls used to store all the things they accumulated for their first home or apartment. He was very proud of his workmanship and took it to a shop in a nearby town to have the finish professionally sprayed on. He was so excited about his present to Janice that he asked Wilma to ride over to see the hope chest while it was at the other shop. Wilma was very impressed with his efforts and complimented him, but on the way back he surprised her with his thoughts.

"Mrs. Hampton, I don't know what to do. I could fight a bear and win, but how can I fight Janice talking to other boys?"

Wilma had no answer for him. She knew that Janice wasn't seeing other boys, so the only explanation for his concern must be jealousy. She tucked that little revelation away and decided that she would just watch and see what else developed with this young man.

Christmas morning came and Janice and Kay got up at 3 a.m. to open their presents. Getting up that early to open their presents was a family tradition that had begun when they were small children. Wilma and Joe also got up and they exchanged all their gifts. W.J. wanted Janice to call him when they opened their presents so that he could come over. He brought her hope chest and stayed the rest of the morning with them. It was one of the best Christmas mornings that Janice had ever had.

W.J.'s home life had never been ideal. He had fallen in love with the Hamptons and all their loving family traditions and gatherings. It was something he had never had but had always longed for. Whenever he was with them, he felt like he belonged to a real family.

*****

As spring approached, Janice and W.J. had been dating for eighteen months. Janice was now sixteen years old and W.J. was twenty-one. He seemed to have calmed down and was welcomed back into the semi-good graces of Joe and Wilma. His anger was under control and their relationship was growing. They started talking about possibly getting married when she graduated the next year, but Janice had reservations. In March 1962, as Janice was finishing her junior year, W.J. joined the Air Force. Many of his friends had been drafted into the Vietnam Conflict. He had decided to enlist before he was drafted, so he would have the choice of which branch of the service he joined. After enlisting, he was sent to Lackland Air Force base in Texas for basic training. Janice thought this might be the opportunity to break up once and for all. She didn't have any desire to be married to someone who would take her away from home to some distant place. Janice decided to not write W.J. while he was gone, but her mama insisted that she keep in contact with him. She felt sorry for him being all alone, and she thought that Janice's letters might be the only contact he had during basic training.

*****

W.J. had been gone six weeks for basic training and Janice was enjoying her freedom. One afternoon she met her friend Sally at the Dairy Bar after school.

"When will W.J. get home?" Sally asked.

Janice sipped on her milkshake before she answered, "I don't know, and I really don't care either. These last six weeks have been wonderful. I feel like I've got my life back."

Gary, Sally's boyfriend, walked in the door.

"Hey, girls, guess who I just saw?" he said as he sat down at the table.

Janice's heart started pounding, "Who?" she asked.

"W.J., he's back home from basic training. He's over at the pool hall. I just thought you might want to know," he said.

Janice was suddenly sick at her stomach. She felt like she might lose her milkshake.

"Sally, I don't feel well. Could you take me home please?" she asked.

They dropped her off at her parents house. They weren't home from work yet, but the doors were always open. Tullahoma was a very safe town and most people never locked their doors, even at night. Janice walked into the living room and W.J. was sitting on the couch waiting for her. She sat and talked to him and realized that she had missed him, even though she had enjoyed not having him around. Life is funny like that sometimes and very confusing.

"I'm going to California for training, and I'll be there for three months. If I study really hard and come out first in my class, then I'll get to pick where I'm assigned. Wouldn't that be great? I think I would pick Florida so that I could be close to my older sister who lives there. What do you think about Florida?" W.J. excitedly asked her.

"I'm sure Florida is nice. Probably a lot hotter than it is here. Why do you want to know what I think about Florida?" She asked, scared of the answer.

"Well, if we get married after you graduate, that's where we will have to live until I'm out of the service," he explained.

W.J. was home for two weeks before leaving for

California. Once there, he worked extremely hard, trying to obtain the first place in his class. On the weekends, his buddies would go across the border into Mexico to party, but W.J. stayed on base spending his time studying. He also spent his time working every chance he got, and he made a sizeable amount of money just ironing his friends' uniforms. W.J. was a hard worker and he never had trouble making or keeping money.

During the three months, Janice wrote to W.J. faithfully. This time, Wilma didn't have to talk her into it, she did it willingly. She liked the idea of having a steady boyfriend, but she also liked the idea of being able to come and go freely without someone to answer to. Maybe this was the best of both worlds. She could have W.J. for a boyfriend, but he was going to be shipped off to some distant base so she wouldn't have to deal with him every day. However, the longer she was away from him, the more she realized that she missed him. By the time the three months was over, she was glad to have him back home.

At the end of the training, W.J. finished first in his class. He chose Homestead Air Force Base in Homestead, Florida. It was very near Miami and his older sister. When he returned to Tullahoma, he decided that he didn't want to wait until Janice graduated to marry her. He couldn't stand the thought of her being in Tullahoma and him being in south Florida.

W.J. asked Joe and Wilma for permission to marry Janice. She was still two months away from being 17. He promised them that she would finish her last year of school in Florida. They were reluctant, but knew if they refused that W.J. and Janice would elope, so they gave their permission.

On September 20, 1962, Janice married W.J.

Chapter 3

Janice and W.J. spent their wedding night at the Holiday Inn in Manchester. They returned home the next day to pack for the move to Florida and started their married life with a twenty-four hour bus trip to Homestead.

Now, a twenty-four hour bus trip is no way to start a marriage. By the time they got to Miami, they were both worn out and irritable. Janice hoped that they could make enough money to never have to ride the bus all the way to or from Tennessee again.

Once in Miami, they stayed with friends for two weeks while searching for an apartment in Homestead. When they settled in their apartment, W.J. was true to his word and Janice enrolled in school. Because she was married, she wasn't allowed to attend a public high school. She had to attend a vocational school that was thirty minutes away by bus. However, the current semester had already started, so she had to wait until January to begin.

The first few weeks of marriage were great. W.J. worked at the Air Force base during the day and Janice learned to cook and keep their small apartment clean.

They had been in Homestead for three weeks when the Cuban Missile Crisis erupted. The Air Force wanted all dependents out of the area and began loading women and children onto planes and flying them to different bases.

Janice had already made a friend named Karen, who was from Nashville. Her husband, along with W.J., wanted their wives to drive back to Tennessee. They were more comfortable with their wives driving than putting them on a plane bound for another Air Force base. They packed them into Karen's car and sent them home to Tennessee. The trip was a long one, even by car, because the route was along state highways that wandered through every little town. Construction on the interstate system had just begun a few years earlier and was years away from being completed. They spent the night in Vidalia, Georgia and drove on to Tullahoma the next day, where Karen dropped Janice off at her parents' house before driving on to her home in Nashville.

Wilma and Joe were still at work, but Janice knew that Kay would be home soon, so she slipped into the house to wait for her. Janice heard her coming in the door and hid to scare her. Kay neared the place where Janice was standing.

"Ahhhh!" screamed Janice as she jumped out in front of Kay.

"Ahhhhhhhh!" Kay screamed in terror.

"Gee, I'm sorry I didn't think I would scare you that bad," Janice apologized as Kay burst into tears.

Kay hugged her, "That's okay. I've cried every day since you got married. Why should today be any different?

What are you doing here?"

"The Air Force evacuated all the dependents because of the Cuban Missile Crisis. I drove up with a friend who lives in Nashville. I'll be home until the crisis is over!"

Janice was at home for almost two weeks. The Cuban Missile Crisis lasted from October 16-28th. Afterwards, the dependents of the military personnel were allowed back onto the base. Karen drove from Nashville to Tullahoma to pick up Janice, then they returned to Homestead.

Before she left, Janice had promised her parents and Kay that she would write them regularly and she did. Because she wrote home so often, she used a lot of envelopes. One day during a shopping trip, she picked up an extra box.

"These are cheaper," W.J. said as he spied a less expensive brand. He took the box from Janice's hand and exchanged it for the cheaper brand.

They finished their shopping and returned home.

"Janice," he said as they unpacked their purchases, "I'm very disappointed in you. You've got to learn to shop economically. It's time for me to spank you."

He grabbed a hair brush and started to hit her very harshly.

"W.J.! That hurts. Please stop," Janice pleaded, but it did no good. He stopped when he was finished. Soon after the hair brush incident, he began to push her whenever he became irritated.

Christmas 1962 was nearing and they had a huge family Christmas planned. Wilma, Joe, Kay, and Mr. and

Mrs. Quick were all driving down to Melbourne, Florida to W.J.'s oldest sister's house. Janice and W.J. arrived and rented a house for the holidays. Wilma, Joe, and Kay stayed with them in the rental house while Mr. and Mrs. Quick stayed with their daughter. This was their first Christmas combining the two families and it was a wonderful time of celebration. Janice couldn't have been happier and she enjoyed being able to spend Christmas with her parents and sister. It made living so far away a little bit easier.

In January, she began school. Her parents sent her $5 each week to help with the bus fare. It was a long ride, but Janice enjoyed the time away from the apartment. It was a challenge to complete her entire senior year in just one semester, but she was determined to succeed. Surprisingly, even though she was around both boys and girls at the vocational school, W.J. never showed any signs of jealousy.

They had been married almost five months, and in February Janice found out she was pregnant. She was ecstatic! A family of her own was what she had always wanted.

The next few months W.J.'s temper grew and surfaced more frequently. Janice was living in a no-win situation. Everything she did irritated him. If she attempted to carry on a conversation, he became upset. If she didn't talk, he became upset. During this time, W.J. went from shoving Janice to kicking her.

Even with the abuse that she was getting at home and being pregnant, somehow she managed to maintain a "B" average and graduate from high school in June of 1963.

Three months after graduation, she was nearing the time to deliver her baby. Two weeks before the baby was due, Wilma traveled to Florida to help Janice. She was excited about her first grandchild and knew that the young mother could use a couple of extra hands in the coming weeks. However, Wilma's employer, whom she had faithfully served for many years, wouldn't let her take time off to travel to Homestead to help Janice. Joe told her to go ahead and turn in her notice, so she did, and she was free to stay as long as Janice needed her.

Wilma took the same bus trip that Janice had the year before and liked it even less than Janice did. She was ill and irritable about the bus ride by the time she arrived in Homestead, complaining about the many stops that the bus made along the way. But she hadn't seen Janice since Christmas, so it was worth all the irritation in the world to be with her.

Janice was having trouble with her feet swelling so they went to a local store, while W.J. was at work, and Janice bought a pair of shoes for $10. When W.J. got home from work, he noticed Janice's new shoes.

"Where did you get those?" he asked.

"I bought them today, because my feet are swelling so much that it's impossible to get my other shoes on," Janice explained.

"You didn't ask me if you could buy those shoes or spend that much money!" he shouted.

W.J. grabbed Janice and started shaking her. Then

he started kicking her. She was trying her best to keep out of reach, but it wasn't easy. It was hard to maneuver when you were nine months pregnant.

Wilma was in shock. She had never encountered anything like this. It was over before she could form the words to protest. Wilma was just devastated to see her daughters living conditions. She followed Janice into the bedroom.

"Janice! I knew that he was verbally abusive. I've heard it myself since I've been here, but how long has he been treating you like this?" Wilma asked.

"For a while," she admitted. It felt good to let someone else know what was happening.

"Why didn't you tell us?" Wilma asked, heartbroken.

"I didn't want to worry you and I figured he would change. Once I found out that I was pregnant, I thought the baby might soften him up and we could be a real family. I love him and I really want this to work," Janice told her mother as she put cold compresses on her legs to try to help with the swelling.

When Janice checked into the hospital to deliver her first child, she had multiple bruises on her legs. It was impossible to hide them from the doctors and nurses but, thankfully, everyone was too busy bringing William Joseph (Joey) into the world to ask what happened. It was September 30, 1963, just over a year from her wedding. It had been a horrible twelve months, but she had survived it and now she had a beautiful baby boy to comfort her.

Janice was very grateful to have her mother with

her. Wilma was an invaluable help after she returned home from the hospital.

"Let's go for a long walk," W.J. suggested her first day home.

"It's a little warm for a walk, and I'm still recovering," Janice explained.

She saw the look in his eyes and changed her mind.

"Okay, let's go for a long walk."

Janice agreed to accompany W.J. whenever he demanded they go on long walks. He was growing more and more resentful of the time that she spent with Joey and it seemed like the only way to ward off his explosive rants was to go with him. He required her undivided attention.

One afternoon, Wilma was holding Joey and standing in the bathroom doorway.

"Put your finger right here," W.J. commanded Wilma pointing to his own arm. "Go ahead put your finger right here on my arm."

She turned and walked away. Wilma felt that he was taunting her to touch him so that he would have an excuse to start abusing her also. She wasn't going to play that game.

While she was in Homestead, Wilma was sleeping in the living room, and the baby's bassinet was also in there. W.J. was adamant that he didn't want the baby in the bedroom because it might awaken him.

"Joey sure is fretful tonight," Wilma remarked.

"Yes, I think I'll stay out here with him for a while," Janice said.

Janice and Joey

Wilma and Joe Hampton

W.J. was already in the bedroom. They sat quietly trying to get Joey settled down. After a while, Janice also fell asleep.

Wilma sat in the semi-darkness thinking about the situation that her daughter and now her grandson were in. It made her furious to think that she and Joe had treated W.J. like their own child. They had grown to love him and this is the way he repaid love? She decided to call her husband and let him know what was going on. She quietly dialed the number and talked as low as she could when he answered.

"Joe, I've been keeping something from you, but I think you ought to know what kind of life your oldest daughter is living. We don't have the good son-in-law that we both thought we had. Well, he's....."

Wilma was interrupted as W.J. came storming out of the bedroom screaming.

Janice and Joey both bolted wide awake at the sound.

"Okay, old woman! You have five minutes to get out of here!!" he screamed.

Wilma jumped and dropped the phone. She picked it up and told Joe she would call him later and immediately started gathering up her things. Janice was still disoriented from sleep and fright, but she and Wilma both knew he meant it and he was capable of great damage to both of them if she didn't move quickly.

W.J. looked at Janice and said, "You better warn your mother not to report this incident to the Base Commander or I'll kill all of you!"

Wilma quickly left to try to defuse the situation. She walked to Janice's friend's apartment in the unit behind them.

"Louise, can I please stay here tonight?" Wilma asked when Louise opened the door.

"Mrs. Hampton, what's wrong?" Louise could see that Wilma had been crying and she was white as a ghost.

"W.J. just exploded again. He gave me five minutes to get out of the house. I need to call my husband to drive down and get me. Will you help me find a hotel for a few days until he gets here?"

Wilma was devastated. It was hard to explain to her husband how horrible Janice's life was. He agreed to start immediately for Miami. It was a two day trip and Louise insisted she stay with her until Joe got there.

By the time Joe arrived in Homestead to get Wilma, Janice had decided to take Joey and drive back to Tullahoma with them. W.J. was not happy.

"She's my wife and I'll do what I want to with her," he informed Joe.

"No, it doesn't work that way," Joe said as he packed his family in the car and drove off.

Wilma and Joe had trusted W.J. with their daughter and they had welcomed him into their home. Now they had to face the fact that they had been completely deceived. There was nothing left inside but an empty sick feeling.

It was a hard two-day trip with Janice recovering from childbirth and a newborn to care for. When they pulled in the driveway, Janice felt a sense of peace. It was good to be back home where she was safe. She was finally able to relax in the knowledge that no one here would hurt her. However, W.J. wasn't going to give up that easily. He started calling immediately saying that he was getting military leave to come to Tennessee.

"Oh no, he won't!" Wilma declared. "I'm calling the base commander and explaining the situation to him. I'll request that W.J. not be given enough leave to come to Tennessee."

She did just that, but it did no good. W.J. was given leave and he took the bus back to Tullahoma. He came straight to the Hampton's home.

Janice was sitting in the house rocking Joey and just happened to look out the window as a yellow cab pulled up in the driveway. W.J. stepped out of it.

Janice shouted, "Mama! W.J. is in the driveway getting out of a cab."

Wilma ran and locked the door. He tried to get in, but couldn't.

"Janice, let me in," he pleaded.

"No, W.J., you can't come in this house!" Wilma shouted back.

"Janice, I love you! Please, come back. I promise I'll never mistreat you again. I'll never hurt you again. I love you. Please, forgive me. Please, come back home with me," W.J. pleaded through the doorway.

Janice walked to the door. She didn't dare open it, but wanted to show him how Joey had grown in the last two weeks. She held the baby up to the glass in the door so that he could see his son. Meanwhile, Wilma had called Mr. and Mrs. Quick to come get W.J. He stayed outside until his parents arrived and then left with them.

For the next 10 days, W.J. regularly went to the Hampton's house to plead with Janice to come back. He wore her resolve down and she agreed to return to Florida. All he had really done was to shake, kick and push her. She was willing to work through his anger to have the ideal family that she had always wanted. W.J.'s parents drove them to the airport in Chattanooga.

When they returned to Homestead, things went well for an entire month, then it all started downhill one afternoon when W.J. couldn't get their car started.

"Janice, come out here and help me push the car," he shouted from the door.

"W.J., I can't come outside to the parking lot and leave Joey in here alone!" she responded.

"Lay him on the couch! He will be fine for ten minutes," he demanded.

"No, I won't leave him in here alone!"

"You'll do as I say," he shouted as he closed the distance between them and slapped her violently.

Her head snapped around and it felt like her eyes were going to jump out of their sockets. She was stunned. The slap he gave her in the car for biting her nails was like a pat on the cheek compared to this. When she finally could focus again, she realized he was dragging her outside to help with the car regardless. She looked back at Joey as she was dragged through the door. He was safely on the couch with a pillow between him and the edge. He might cry, but he wouldn't get hurt.

It seemed like he got confidence from rough handling her. Confidence that he could have his way whenever he wanted because, after the incident with the car, the kicking and pushing started again with a vengeance.

Then one evening two month old Joey began crying. He was colicky and very fretful.

"W.J., would you please hold the baby while I go into the kitchen and fix him a bottle?" Janice asked.

While she was in the kitchen, she heard him start to cry harder. She entered the living room and found W.J. shaking Joey.

Janice ran over to him and started hitting W.J. on the back.

"STOP SHAKING HIM!" she screamed as she continued to hit him.

W.J. laid Joey on the couch and grabbed Janice. He repeatedly threw her against the concrete walls of the apartment. He showed no mercy. By the time he left for work, Janice was seriously hurt but W.J. did not touch Joey again that night.

Janice held Joey and cried. She tried her best to doctor herself, but this was so much more than shaking, kicking, and pushing. Even if she could heal the outside wounds, that was only half the battle. Nothing she could do would heal the emotional wounds inside her. It didn't take long to decide to call her parents.

"Hi, Mama. I just wanted you to know that W.J. is still beating me and tonight I caught him shaking Joey. I don't know what to do," she sobbed.

"Is the baby okay?" Wilma asked.

"I think so, he's acting normal."

"When will W.J. be home from work?"

"He's working the 3-11 p.m. shift today, why?" Janice asked.

"You've got to get out of there. Go to one of your neighbors, borrow some money, and then get yourself and the baby on a plane and get home!" Wilma told her. "I'll call my step sister in Miami and have her come pick you up. Pack now Janice. Don't wait any longer. I'll tell her to pick you up in one hour."

Wilma's step-sister took Janice and Joey to the airport before W.J. returned home from work. When the plane was taxiing down the runway, Janice finally exhaled.

Janice, Joey, and W.J.

CHAPTER 4

Downward Spiral

This time at home started out no differently than the last separation. W.J.'s phone calls began immediately and continued relentlessly. But Janice did not give in, and she and Joey stayed with her parents for four months. It was a wonderful time of rest and security for her. Wilma and Joe enjoyed the time they had with their daughter and their first grandchild. In April 1964, Janice finally agreed to return to Florida. She was hoping that the longer separation had given W.J. plenty of time to contemplate his actions and attitude. W.J. had given up their apartment and moved onto the Air Force base when Janice left. Before they returned, he rented another apartment. Although she was hoping for a change, the cycle continued once they were back in Homestead with beatings followed by repentant vows to never do it again.

W.J. was working a second job in his spare time. He returned to his high school part time profession, working for a moving company. Janice was glad for the extra time alone on the weekends. It seemed that the less he was home, the less she got hurt.

That summer, W.J. got two weeks leave and they

drove home to surprise everyone. The Hamptons were thrilled to see their first grandchild crawling. Janice and W.J. also visited his parents, but stayed at the Hamptons'. They had a great two weeks, and there was no abuse of any kind so Janice hated to see the vacation come to an end. Eventually, they started the long drive back.

As they neared Atlanta, W.J. asked her, "Would you like to drive for a while so that I can rest?"

"Yes, I would love to drive," Janice answered him excited at the ideal of being able to help.

She got behind the wheel and took off down the road. There's a certain freedom that driving gives you. She felt safe and secure when she knew that she was in control, at least temporarily. She drove for a while before W.J. spotted a rest area.

"Pull over in that rest area," he commanded.

When she started to slow down, she hit the brakes a little harder than he wanted. He was furious and started hitting her while she was still trying to get the car off the road safely.

"If you don't stop beating me, I'm gonna turn this car around and head back to Tullahoma!" she screamed between blows.

He stopped the beating but he took over driving and continued on to Homestead.

Just before Joey had his first birthday, something happened that eclipsed all the other beatings. Janice exercised a little independence only to regret it for days afterward. The argument was over nothing in particular, like it was most every time.

"I told you to quit back talking me!" W.J. screamed in rage. He lashed out and hit Janice in the face.

She looked him square in the eyes and said, "A real man doesn't beat a woman."

"You better take that back, woman, or you will pay dearly for it." He glared at her, waiting for her to apologize.

She refused.

He started beating her, continuing on and off for three days. The next-door neighbor, who had out of town guests, heard the beatings. He stood outside their door and shouted, "If you don't stop beating her, I'm going to call the police!" But, he never did.

During a lull in the beatings on the third day, Janice went outside the apartment for some reason. Another neighbor, who was also regularly getting beaten by her husband, saw her. She was shocked at the state that Janice was in and insisted on taking her to the hospital on the Air Force base.

"You can't take Joey. He will stay here with me," W.J. informed her.

"No, I want to take him with me," Janice pleaded.

W.J. took her off to the side, "If you tell the hospital that I did this to you, I'll take Joey and leave and you'll never see us again."

She and the neighbor waited to see the doctor at the hospital. He was shocked when he saw her condition.

"What happened to you, Mrs. Quick?" the doctor asked.

"I walked into a door," Janice lied, not realizing

that she had finger mark bruises on her neck.

"I see," was all he said as he doctored her many wounds. He asked no further questions the entire time. As she stood to leave, he said, "Next time, please bring a picture of yourself with you so that I will know what you really look like."

When she returned home, she got up enough nerve to look at herself in the mirror. The doctor's comment wasn't surprising. Her face was so swollen out of proportion that, if you had never met her, you would have no idea what she looked like.

It was soon September and they celebrated Joey's first birthday. W.J. got him a little red wagon and he seemed genuinely excited to give it to him. He hadn't abused Joey since the shaking incident when he was two months old.

Autumn marched on with no changes in W.J.'s behavior. He began beating her once and she tried to escape. She made it outside the apartment but he was right behind her. As he picked her up and threw her over his shoulder, she saw some of her neighbors sitting in lawn chairs just a few feet away.

"Call the police! He's going to kill me," she begged as he returned her to the apartment and to the beating. They did nothing.

Christmas was approaching and Janice found out that she was pregnant again. She had a fourteen-month old, an abusive husband, a one bedroom apartment and another baby on the way. If you could take the word abusive from her husband's description, Janice would have been happy. She had always wanted a family of her own. With the new baby on the way, they moved into a two bedroom apartment. To Janice, this was a big step, an acknowledgement of their growing family. Surely, this meant that things were getting better.

It was February 12, 1965 and she was two and a half months along in her pregnancy. Before W.J. left for work that Friday night, he was in a violent mood and he started hitting Janice.

"No, W.J., the baby, the baby!" Janice screamed in fear.

He didn't respond to her. He just knocked her to the floor and kicked her in the stomach. Janice rolled over in pain and tried to turn her back to him to protect the baby. He kicked her in the back then he left for work.

She lay there a while until the pain subsided, then got up and went about taking care of Joey and the house. Later that night after Joey was in bed, she made W.J. his favorite cookies, peanut butter. She wanted to let him know that she forgave him and that she loved him. When she went to bed, her stomach was cramping a little but she didn't think there was anything to worry about. Early the next morning, she started bleeding.

"W.J.," she said as she gently shook her sleeping husband. "Wake up. Something's wrong."

"What's the matter?" he asked as he sat up.

"I'm bleeding. I think I need to go to the hospital," she told him.

W.J. got up as Janice carried a sleepy Joey to a friend's house. As they started to the hospital, the pains increased from stomach cramps to labor pain. Ironically, it bothered him to see her in pain. He sat with her in the hospital while they treated her. Since husbands weren't allowed in the delivery rooms, W.J. had not seen Janice go through labor with Joey. This time, he was seeing plenty of labor. W.J. kept watching her in genuine concern as the labor pains increased.

"Honey, you've aborted your baby," the nurse said as she took Janice's hand.

"Oh no ma'am. I would never have an abortion!" Janice innocently answered.

"No dear, that's not what I meant. I'm very sorry to tell you this, but you miscarried your baby." She left the room for a few minutes, then returned to prep her for surgery.

As she entered the surgical procedure room, Janice thought of her Mother. It was February 13, 1965, Wilma's birthday. Under the anesthesia, Janice kept saying, 'I want my Mama'.

*****

In June 1965, Janice got a surprise. Wilma, Joe and Kay came to visit her. She and Kay were like two teenagers together again.

"You've met someone?" Janice excitedly asked.

"Yes, I met him last month. His name is Kenneth and he is wonderful," Kay said. "I think I've fallen in love with him already!"

Kay, like Janice, had always wanted a family. She had been out of high school for a year and was enrolled in the local beauty school. The week that her family visited was the best time Janice had since getting married. They went to the local parks, visited alligator preserves, walked the nature trails and generally had a wonderful time. The week went by way too fast for Janice.

"Do you really have to go?" Janice asked her parents.

"Yes, Janice. You know your dad only has two weeks off. It takes two days to get back home and he will only have a couple of days to rest up before starting back to work. I wish you could come with us," Wilma told her.

"Yeah, why don't you leave that maniac and come back home? You know we love you and will take care of you," Kay commented.

"I don't want to leave. I'm still hoping for a good marriage. I'm sure things will get better," Janice told them.

As usual, Kay spoke her mind, "Crazy people don't get better!"

After they said their goodbyes and left, Janice cried for hours, missing them already.

In the middle of the summer, Janice found out she was expecting her third baby. She was excited, but determined that this baby would not suffer the same fate as the last one. At the beginning of September, she received a letter from Kay. Kenneth had popped the question. They would be marrying by the end of the month and Kay wanted her to be in the wedding.

Janice was so excited for her only sister. Of course she wanted to be there for her, but in reality, there was only a slim chance that she could.

photo provided by Kim and Jada

Janice and Kay

photo provided by Kim and Jada

Kenneth and Kay's Wedding

Janice waited until W.J. was in a good mood to talk to him about Kay's wedding. She was nervous all day just imagining all the possible scenarios when she told him, but the time had come and she couldn't put it off any longer.

"W.J., I have some good news to tell you," she started apprehensively.

"What good news?" he asked uninterested.

"Kenneth asked Kay to marry him. They are getting married this month. I would really like to be there, if that's okay with you," she managed to get that much said before he exploded.

"I don't want another son-in-law in this family! You get on that phone and you call Kay and tell her that she cannot get married!" W.J. bellowed.

"What?! You've got to be kidding. I'm not going to call her and tell her any such thing. Why would you even say anything like that?"

He answered her with his fist, like he did so many times. The next day dawned and Janice's left arm was badly bruised from his abuse.

"You are not going to kill this baby! I'm going home," she announced

"Fine, but you're not taking Joey," he informed her.

"Oh, yes I am," Janice said.

They argued back and forth for a while, but she ended the argument when she declared, "We will not be back."

"Mama, I'm coming home," Janice said into the phone right in front of W.J..

"Okay, just call me back with the flight times when you get them," her mama answered breathing a sigh of relief.

Janice called the airlines but couldn't get a flight until the next day. That night, she slept in their room with Joey, and W.J. slept in the other bedroom.

Strangely enough, W.J. agreed to drive her to the airport.

"Janice, please don't go. I promise I won't ever hit you again. Don't you know that I love you? I promise that I will change. You'll see. Just please don't leave me," he pleaded.

She had seen this act before and realized that there was some part down deep that was sincere, but the monster that was in control the majority of the time didn't listen to the part down deep.

"I won't chance losing this child because you can't control your temper. And no, I don't know that you love me. If you loved me, you wouldn't abuse me. You have a very strange definition of the word love," she said. Janice took the chance to speak her mind relying on the fact that he wouldn't hit her in public and that she wouldn't see him for a long while.

Upon arriving at the airport, Janice, with Joey in hand, proceeded to the check-in counter. W.J. followed close behind them. After checking in, they made their way through the airport arriving at the boarding gate. As Janice and Joey were about to enter the gate, W.J. grabbed Joey and took off running.

"Help! Help! He's got my baby!" She shouted as

she ran after W.J.

Two security guards heard her screams and looked up at a determined W.J. running straight towards them. They both grabbed him and removed Joey from his arms. They returned Joey to Janice and detained W.J. while she boarded the plane. She was wearing a sleeveless dress and the security guards would have seen her bruises. Her bruises were also the first thing that her parents saw as she exited the plane in Nashville.

Her time at home was wonderful, although it took several months to completely relax. The first few weeks, every time the phone rang, she would have a mild panic attack. But, W.J. left her alone.

Wilma and Joe enjoyed the time they had with their grandson. He was a typical two year old and entertained them endlessly. Kay also got to know her nephew. She was starting her married life, but still had time to spend with Janice and Joey.

After a couple of months, Janice realized that she was breathing again. She felt like she was always holding her breath around her husband, but here she could breathe the clear air of freedom. And it did feel like freedom; freedom from pain, freedom from fear, freedom from stress. The only thing she wasn't free from was the disappointment of her life. She had dreamed of a storybook life with a family that closely resembled the family in which she was raised. But, in reality, her life was nothing like the way she was raised. Her dad had hardly ever raised his voice to his wife, much less his hand. How could she have chosen someone that was so different from what she wanted? It embarrassed her for people to know how badly she had been deceived. The only comfort that she had was realizing that even her parents had been deceived. If W.J. was a good enough actor to deceive them, then maybe she wasn't as stupid as she felt. Stupid or not, it was what it was...a nightmare life.

About the time she started to relax, it was Christmas, and W.J. had military leave. He made his way to Tullahoma and spent Christmas at the Hampton's. At first Janice was anxious about spending time with W.J. but, once again, while he was with the Hamptons, he behaved himself. It was a good Christmas, but, as Janice was learning, whenever he wasn't in a rage, everything was good. If only she was married to the man that everybody else saw. W.J. left right after the holidays and traveled back to Homestead.

The further away she got from the abuse, the more she started to hope that maybe things would change this time. She didn't trust this hope, but it was all she had. Three more months passed and the time came to deliver her second child. On March 2, 1966, Jason Brent was born.

W.J., Janice, Joey, and Jason

Chapter 5

Storm Clouds Gather

Shortly after Jason was born, W.J.'s military service was finished and he returned to Tullahoma. After returning, he was hired at AEDC (Arnold Engineering Development Center), which was part of the Arnold Air Force Base. He was working in the steam plant, but later moved to a technician position in the Von Karman Gas Dynamics Facility.

"Janice I promise you I've changed! I've missed you and Joey so much. My life is nothing without you. Please come back to me and let's make this marriage work. Please. I love you so much. I realize that now. I won't ever hurt you again. We've got two sons and they need their father in their lives," W.J. pleaded regularly with Janice to come back to him.

"I guess we could try it again," Janice finally conceded. He did seem more sincere this time and she was willing to give the hope that had grown in her for the last eight months a chance to bloom.

"Let's buy a house. I'm making good money and apartment living is not easy for a growing family. Joey and Jason need a yard they can run and play in. Would you like a house?" W.J. asked.

"Okay, we'll start looking for a house."

While they looked for their own house, W.J. moved in to Joe and Wilma's home with Janice. This was different than last Christmas. W.J. started showing his true nature to other people and she was constantly playing referee between W.J. and her parents, W.J. and Kay, and W.J. and the children. His irritability, hatefulness and screaming at Joey, was pushing everyone to the edge. One day Kay walked in when he was holding three-year-old Joey, screaming at him. She ran up to him, jerked Joey out of his arms, ran to a bedroom and locked herself and the baby in the room. She had become very fond of her nephew and was determined to protect him from abuse. By the end of their first month with Janice's parents, Wilma had enough, and told them they had to move out. She could not stand W.J.'s verbal abuse one day longer.

Their search brought them to a new subdivision. The house they fell in love with was a three bedroom ranch house that was almost complete. It had a big yard for the boys to play in and plenty of room to grow their expanding family. Life in their new house started out well. For a short period, W.J. backed off of the beatings and was just slapping and pushing Janice around periodically. This fostered the hope that had been growing in Janice. She was praying that the change of life, from military to civilian, was just what W.J. needed to break this abusive cycle. It worked for a while, but he soon fell back into the same old patterns that had haunted her for the past four years.

At the same time, Janice was uncovering some family information about W.J. that she had failed to learn before they married. He came from a violent, abusive home. His dad was also a wife beater. But the violent nature and traumatic lifestyle didn't only come from his dad's side of the family. Although his mother never abused him, her mother (W.J.'s grandmother) was beaten to death by her second husband. W.J.'s mother had married at the young age of fourteen. She had witnessed her own mother being beaten many times and she found herself in the same situation. Her husband, W.J.'s father, abused her throughout their entire married life. W.J. witnessed his mother being beaten on many occasions and yet, she never attempted to leave. She said she had no other place to go. Once when W.J. was a teenager, he slapped his mother hard enough that he left her face bruised. His father's response was, "I suppose she needed that!"

W.J.'s father also abused W.J. and his siblings. W.J. was regularly left in charge of the farm while his dad and older brother traveled for work. At an early age, he was expected to plow, cultivate and harvest the large farm. If the results weren't what his dad was expecting, W.J. paid for it with a beating.

*****

During the next year, Janice set about to make their house a home. She enjoyed the life of taking care of the children, cooking and cleaning. If it wasn't for W.J.'s abusive actions, she would have had the perfect life. Some weeks actually went along perfectly, other weeks were a nightmare. The pendulum was swinging faster and faster; from very good to very bad.

Most of the beatings were for what W.J. called 'talking back'. He frequently came home in a combative mood. Something at work had set him off, either his job or his co-workers. He would wait for any slight comment from Janice that would push him deeper into his rage. Inevitably, she would say something that he could twist or blame her for and the beatings would begin.

Outwardly, they were a happy couple. Inwardly, nothing had changed. Well actually, one thing changed. In Tullahoma, W.J. was more careful about where he hit Janice. He avoided hitting her around the neck or face. He simply hit her on the body where her clothes would cover up the bruises. Most of the time Janice wore long sleeve blouses and high collars to hide all the black and blue spots.

Occasionally, W.J. showed remorse when he saw Janice in her nightgown. The bruises were much more apparent then. Several times he started crying and vowed that he would never beat her again. Of course, that statement along with his regretfulness, was always short-lived. Yet W.J. was very conscientious of what people in Tullahoma knew and thought about him and his family. His older brother had a serious wreck in 1966 and the papers reported that he was severely intoxicated. W.J. was mortified that the community would know that his brother was an alcoholic.

In contrast, Janice's family was well thought of in the community. Joe and Wilma were both active in their church and served in various social groups. Kay and Kenneth were both working and enjoying their early married life. Kay, who was ready to deliver her first child, stopped by one day to see her sister. She, Janice, Kenneth, and W.J. were standing in the driveway talking. The garage door was open and Joey was inside playing.

"Has Kenneth ever told you whether he wants a girl or boy?" Janice asked.

"No, he said it doesn't matter to him. I told him it was a good thing he didn't want a boy, since I'm certain this child is a girl," Kay smiled.

"You're just saying that because you always wanted a girl. What are you going to do if it's a boy?" Janice teased her.

"I'll bring him over here. You'll never notice one more boy," she laughed.

There was a noise from inside the garage as if Joey had knocked something over.

"I'm gonna wear that kid out!" W.J. bellowed as he turned to start into the garage. Janice ran to retrieve Joey before W.J. could get to him.

Kay sprang into action. She grabbed a two-by-four which was laying on the edge of the driveway and started into the garage.

"I'm going to kill that S.O.B.!" Kay screamed in anger.

She lunged at a stunned W.J. with the two-by-four as Kenneth grabbed her from the back.

"Drop the two-by-four, Kay," Kenneth said, as he held her firmly around her large belly. "Come on Kay, I'm not going to let you hit him."

She fought Kenneth to get to W.J. After a struggle, Kenneth won and removed the board from Kay's hands. He led her to the car and they left.

W.J. walked over to Janice. He was visibly shaken.

"I think she was going to kill me," he said.

"Yep, she was," Janice agreed as she walked past him into the house.

Despite the chaos of home, Janice and W.J. were very active in their church. They attended the small Baptist church where Janice and Kay were raised. Janice taught the teenage Sunday school class and W.J. helped with whatever needed to be done in the church. No one except the immediate family, ever suspected what was going on in their home. All the church members loved W.J. He was always kind and respectful, always willing to help with any task, and always there with his family.

Janice had one Sunday school student named Jerry. He was a typical 17 year old, but he had recently contracted meningitis. Jerry was a tough kid but there were several times that the disease almost took his life.

"Janice, I just got word about Jerry," the lady in charge of the church prayer line told Janice on the phone one day. "He's taken a turn for the worse. The doctors don't think he's going to make it this time."

Janice hung up the phone and sat at the kitchen table crying. Six-year-old Joey and three-year-old Jason heard the noise and came to investigate.

"What's wrong, Mama?" Joey asked.

"Well, you know that Jerry has been very sick. The

doctors don't think he's going to be alive much longer. He's about to go live with Jesus," Janice said through the tears.

Joey and Jason turned and walked out of the kitchen. They walked down the hall to their bedroom, knelt by their beds and prayed for Jerry. Within ten minutes, the phone rang again.

"Janice, you won't believe it! They called to tell us that Jerry has suddenly improved! He's turned a big corner and the doctors are giving him a good chance of making it now!" the prayer line lady exclaimed.

"Thank God!" Janice said, laughing in relief.

Joey and Jason ran back into the kitchen to see what all the laughing was about.

"They just called to say that something big has changed and Jerry will probably live now. He's going to be alright!" she explained.

Joey and Jason started jumping up and down shouting.

"Mama, we went in our room and prayed for Jerry and Jesus heard our prayers and made him well," they shouted in childlike exuberance.

Even with the horrific life that these two children lived in most of the time, their child-like faith was boundless.

*****

In July of 1970, W.J. was one of hundreds laid off at AEDC. In addition to his full-time job, he had been working part time for several years at Couch's, a local store that sold and repaired small appliances. About the time that W.J. was laid off, Couch's decided to get out of the appliance business. W.J. still had work because they honored their service contracts for the appliances that had been sold previously, but he also started getting calls from the general public for in-home appliance repair. His ability with appliance repair and his business sense birthed Quick's Appliance Service. W.J. bought a surplus telephone company truck to work from and began a successful business.

Kenneth wanted to develop a 'brother-in-law' relationship with W.J., so he offered to go out on service calls with him to assist with appliance repairs. As they left the home of a service call one day, W.J. accidently backed his truck into a tree. He was instantly mad.

"I can't believe this! I'm going to go straight home and beat Janice!" He screamed in rage.

"W.J., now there's no need for that. Janice didn't have anything to do with you backing into that tree. You don't need to beat her," Kenneth protested.

"Are you kidding me? How can you live with a woman and not beat her?!" W.J. asked Kenneth, in all seriousness.

About the time that W.J. was laid off from AEDC, Janice found out she was pregnant with their third child. This pregnancy was no easier than the others because W.J.'s beatings never stopped. When Janice went to the hospital to deliver, W.J. warned her to hide the huge bruise on her arm. He threatened her, 'You better not tell anyone where that bruise came from'.

Despite all the trauma inflicted on her body by her

husband, she delivered Julie Dawn, a healthy baby girl born on February 14, 1971.

W.J. doted on Julie from the beginning. It appeared that she was the only person on earth who could move him to express some form of love. In a very strange way, at times, he actually showed signs of a protecting father with Julie. During one of his many fits of rage, W.J. literally destroyed Julie's crib. When he saw her standing in the doorway, watching her crib being dismantled, he told Janice, 'Get her out of here!' He evidently didn't want her to be upset. He went immediately and purchased another crib. The matter was never brought up again.

In the early summer of 1972, their church was having revival. The young evangelist was someone that Janice had known most of her life. She sat in the service that night completely engulfed in what he was preaching. She was under such pressure and stress that she could not think straight most of the time. Her world was always upside down and the trauma that Janice endured was taking a toll on her mind. *Would I be going through all of this if I truly knew the Lord as my Savior?* At the end of the service, Janice went to the altar to pray. She had to know that she was really a child of God. She prayed and felt the reassurance of the Lord that she was indeed His. The peace that she so desperately needed flooded her troubled soul. She didn't know it at the time, but the peace and reassurance that she received from the Lord that night was the only way she would mentally survive the coming months.

Later that summer, Janice's friend, Maxine, called

Jason, Joey, Janice, and Julie
Easter 1971

Joey, Jason, and Julie
May 1971

the house one day. She had a bumper crop of tomatoes and called to see if Janice wanted any. W.J. answered the phone.

"W.J., where's Janice?" Maxine asked.

"Oh, she's around here somewhere," W.J. answered.

Maxine thought that was an unusual answer for him. Usually, he would take the phone directly to Janice when she called.

"Well, we have a huge crop of tomatoes and I was wondering if y'all would like some."

"No, I don't think so," W.J. said,

"Okay. Where is Janice?" she asked again.

"Oh, she's cleaning out a closet," W.J. answered.

"Well, have her call me if she wants some," she said as she hung up the phone, perplexed.

W.J. wasn't about to let Maxine talk to Janice right then because he was in the middle of beating her. For some unknown reason, he stopped long enough to answer the phone. Later that day, Kay called Maxine and told her that W.J. had almost killed Janice earlier. Maxine got so upset when she realized the beating might have been going on when she called that she had to leave work.

That day, W.J. beat Janice to the point that one of her legs turned black almost immediately. Usually, Janice treated herself or just left her bruises untreated to heal on their own. But this time she was scared. Kay made her an appointment with Dr. Charles Harvey, a local physician.

When Dr. Harvey entered the examination room, he stopped in his tracks. He stood and looked at her a few minutes.

"Exactly what were you hit with?" he asked Janice in a very firm voice. Dr. Harvey was an excellent doctor who truly cared about his patients, but he was no-nonsense and didn't tolerate foolish behavior. He was stunned at the extent of Janice's beating.

"I know what you're thinking and you're right. I've been beaten. As a matter of fact, this is nowhere near the first time that I've been beaten."

Having summoned the courage to confide in Dr. Harvey that she was an abused wife, she decided that she had enough courage to leave W.J. A couple of days later, she informed him of her plans. He turned and walked out of the house.

Janice packed several days worth of clothes for her and the children. She left the house and went straight to the bank to withdraw cash. Then she drove 70 miles to Nashville and got a hotel room. As soon as she arrived she called her mother.

"Mama, I just wanted you to know that we are somewhere safe," Janice told her. "I'm not going to tell you where, because I don't want you to have to lie to W.J.. I'm sure he will call you and pump you for information."

"He already has so please don't tell me where; I just want to know that you and the children are safe," Wilma said.

"We are safe and we are having a nice time not worrying about him. I'll call you when I head back to Tullahoma," she told Wilma.

The kids had a great time in the hotel swimming pool that night. The next day she took them to Opryland. The amusement park had opened in May and this was their first time to experience it. What a treat that was for her and the children. They weren't constantly worrying what W.J. would do when he found them. They knew there was no way he could know where they were.

They also visited one of Janice's cousins that lived in Nashville. It was great to have time to visit family members that had always been close to her. She had lost touch with everyone since she married, because W.J. never wanted her to have friends.

After a few days, Janice knew she needed to return to Tullahoma. She packed them all up and headed home. The children were quieter on the way back. They knew that W.J. wouldn't take their leaving very well. Janice parked her car at a local elementary school next door to her parents house. They walked over to Wilma and Joe's. Wilma was about to leave for the grocery store so they all went with her. When they arrived back home, W.J. was waiting in the Hampton's driveway holding a concrete block.

"Get out of the car, Janice," he screamed with the concrete block poised to be thrown. "If you don't, I'm throwing this through the window!"

His threat rang hollow when he saw Julie in the car. He lowered the block not wanting to take the chance of hitting her. Janice got out of the car and W.J. began threatening her without ceasing. Weary of the drama, Joe called the police. They arrived fairly quickly since the Hampton home was only eight blocks from the police station.

After assessing the situation, they asked Janice, "Do you want him arrested?"

"Yes," Janice said.

"Then everyone needs to get in their vehicles and we will follow you to the police department to file the complaint," the police instructed.

Janice, Wilma, Joe and the children drove to the police station with W.J. following them.

"Is this going to be in the newspapers?" W.J. asked as they all entered the police department.

"Yes, it will be in the arrest report," the policeman in charge answered.

W.J. asked if he could talk to Janice in private for a few minutes. The officer agreed and he, the Hamptons and the children left the room.

"What is it, W.J.?" she asked, frustrated. She realized that his anger had calmed to the point that he wasn't going to hit her, at least not in the police station.

W.J. looked her coldly in the eyes and said, "If you go through with this, I will kill you, your parents, Kay, and Kenneth."

Fear is a powerful emotion.

They all left without filing the complaint.

The police did tell W.J. to stay away from his home that night. Janice and the children were returning to the house with a promise from the police that they would check on them later in the evening. When the patrol car stopped at the Quick's house, it was W.J. who answered the door. He told the police that everything was okay, and they left without further investigation.

W.J. left soon after the police did, but informed Janice before he left that he would be back at 6:30 a.m. to kill her. That night nine-year-old Joey went to bed with a knife under his pillow. Six-year-old Jason slept with a pair of scissors.

W.J. returned at the appointed time the next morning. He was surprised to see that Janice had not run away. She knew that his threat the night before had not been idle words. If she wanted to keep her parents out of danger, she would have to stay put. There was no place to run. Janice thought that he seemed to be in a better frame of mind than the night before, and then he spoke.

"I'm not going to kill you....this time."

The frustrating part of the abuse was there was no one to help. Going to the authorities was useless. During the 1960s through the early 1970s, domestic abuse was not considered a criminal offense. It was thought of as something in the family that needed to stay in the family. Very rarely did the police arrest a man for beating his wife, and in the rare case that they did, he was usually released quickly. Having an abusive husband arrested was not often in the best interest of the wife. The beating that came after he returned home was hardly worth the pitiful attempt at justice. Janice's case was no different. That's why there was no comfort at all to her that the Chief of Police lived only a block away from their new house.

Even though it was no help to have the authorities close by, the Quicks did have very good neighbors all around them, however, none of them were aware of the situation in which she and the children lived. Right next door lived Bonnie and Billy. They were a good Christian couple raising their own two children; their daughter was the same age as Joey and their son was a few months younger than Jason. The children often played outside together. One afternoon Bonnie was sitting in the swing in the backyard when W.J. came home from work. She waved hello at him and he walked over to where she was swinging. She was just watching her children play in the yard so he sat down in the swing to talk for a few minutes.

"Bonnie, you wouldn't believe what I put up with," W.J. started the conversation. "Janice is so immature. Have you noticed how childlike she is?"

"No, W.J., I haven't noticed," Bonnie said, a little confused at the path the conversation was taking.

"I have to discipline her just like a child. That's how immature she is. Would you believe she left the closet door open at least an inch?! Just left it standing open like that!" He complained, obviously aggravated at Janice's careless actions.

"Well, W.J., I leave my closet doors open all spring and fall so the air can circulate through the clothes," Bonnie answered, surprised at his complaint. He didn't have anything else to say about Janice to Bonnie.

For months, Janice had been trying to think of something that W.J. and the boys could do together to improve their relationship. She remembered that her husband had told her about all the fun he had as a kid going deer hunting with his dad. Deer hunting. Maybe that was one thing that he could do again and enjoy teaching the boys. So, with this quest guiding her decision, for Christmas 1973, she bought W.J. a deer rifle. It wasn't long before she regretted that decision.

One afternoon, W.J. came home from work in a foul mood. He paced around in the kitchen asking her all sorts of questions. She knew what was coming. Anything she said, or didn't say, would light the fuse for another explosion. True to form, W.J. started hitting Janice. After knocking her around the room a couple of times, he loaded the gun.

Handing it to her, he said, "If you don't kill me right now, I'll kill you." Janice took the gun. *What was he up to? Could he truly be admitting that he didn't want to eventually kill her and the only way he could see out was for her to kill him? Was he wanting to commit suicide, but found it to be a cruel last abuse to have Janice do it for him?* Her mind reeled with the possibilities. She was raised in a Christian home and her personal faith and values prevented her from being able to take his life. She just could not shoot her husband. Janice handed him back the gun.

He grabbed it and walked away. That terrifying event prompted her to hide the ammunition immediately. Later that night, W.J. was storming around the house looking for the shells for the rifle.

"Where did you hide the shells?" he screamed.

She didn't answer.

"I said, where did you hide the shells? Tell me right now!"

She didn't answer.

W.J. started beating Janice. Every blow landed with the question 'where did you hide them?', but she wouldn't tell him where they were. As the abuse continued and he became more and more enraged, Janice was fearing for her life. Out of sheer desperation, she eventually answered his repeated question.

"They're in the drawer with my underwear," she gasped in unbearable pain.

He ran to the bedroom and retrieved the ammunition. He loaded the gun and situated himself on the end of the couch. He was holding the rifle in one hand and a bottle of Jack Daniel's in the other.

"Sit down," he ordered her as he pointed to the other end of the couch.

She got up out of the floor where she had landed after the last blow from W.J. and slowly made her way to the couch.

"If you so much as move or even breathe hard, I'll kill you!"

Janice sat at the other end of the couch with the gun pointed at her all night. It was then that she realized she had lost all love for W.J. She had, at one time, truly loved him. That was the only way she withstood the beatings. Through all the years of abuse, Janice had held on to a hope, a hope that W.J. would one day revert to the confident, loving man with whom she had originally fallen in love. She wasn't even sure when she stopped loving him, but it was some time in the last eleven years. Sitting on the end of the couch that night, Janice realized that her desire for a happy, wonderful marriage was definitely not going to happen. She had endured enough. Divorce was inevitable and she knew that she had to get herself and her children out of this impossible, violent life. Janice had tried for years to shield the children from W.J.'s abuse. She would try to keep them away from him when he was in a rage. Sometimes she would drop them off at a friend's house, or send them to bed early to keep them off his radar. But now, after eleven years of relentless abuse, she realized the only way to stay out of range of his anger was to simply not be there.

Once the decision was made, and the spark of hope had gone out completely, Janice felt dead on the inside. Yet she couldn't concentrate on that. She had a plan to form and a family to protect. She would have to step her way through this carefully. In the culture of the 1960s and 70s, no one was supportive of divorce. Her parents would always be there for her, but there was a world of people around her who would disagree with her decision. However, they didn't live with W.J. All the people in their lives, except for a very few, saw the W.J. that he wanted them to see. He was well liked at his job, at church and everywhere that he had connections. They all thought he was a wonderful man, a devoted husband and dad. This was not going to be easy.

A few days later, driving down the road with the children, Joey innocently said, "Why don't we divorce daddy?" That was all the confirmation she needed.

The worst part about this time in their family history was that the abuse didn't stop with Janice. By 1969, W.J. had started abusing six-year-old Joey. While working at Couch's and doing his own service calls, W.J. would often take Joey with him on appliance deliveries or on service calls. He expected Joey to know all the tools of his trade and to be able to hand him the correct one every time. If the correct tool wasn't supplied upon W.J.'s request, Joey would get hit. Sometimes he would get hit in the head, sometimes he would get pushed off of porches or down steps. It started small, but just like his abuse to Janice, it didn't stay small and it didn't stay confined to just Joey.

Jason, Julie, and Joey
Summer 1971

Jason, Julie, and Joey
Fall 1971

Chapter 6

Joey and Jason

Joey heard his dad's truck coming down the street. There was no mistaking that truck. It had a particular engine sound and the way the tires sounded on the pavement struck fear into his young heart. He and Jason ran around the house to hide from W.J.

When they heard him enter the back door, they ran through the front door and tried to make it to their bedroom before he knew they had been playing outside. You just never knew what would set him off. Hiding in their bedroom they tried to judge the mood he was in by what they heard.

"How's my little girl?" W.J. said as he picked Julie up and swung her around in the air. "Have you been a good girl today?"

"Yes, daddy, I been good girl," Julie answered. She had just turned three and was becoming quite the talker.

Julie always put W.J. in a good mood. Unlike his sons, he doted on her. For the time being, Julie was safe from his anger. Joey worried that as she grew, she would become a victim of his rage too. He was determined to protect her at all cost.

"Do you think he's gonna whip us tonight?" seven year old Jason asked with a quivery voice.

"I don't think so. He sounds like he's in a pretty good mood. Do you want to go into the kitchen to see when dinner will be ready? I'm getting hungry."

"No. I don't want to do anything that might make him mad," Jason answered.

"Okay. I'll slip down the hall and see what's going on," Joey said as he quietly left the bedroom.

He was always reluctant to voluntarily have anything to do with W.J. He thought about the time when he was in the first grade. Joey was learning to tell time so W.J. thought he would test him. It was almost bedtime and the clock read 8:45. W.J. had asked Joey to tell him the time. Joey was instantly frightened. He looked at the clock and was adding up in his head what time it was, but the minute hand wasn't on a number that he could quickly count to. He evidently didn't answer fast enough for his dad, because W.J. punched the six year old in the stomach. That was the first time Joey could remember being hit with anything other than W.J.'s belt.

He sure didn't want a beating tonight, but you never could tell when one was coming. He slipped further down the hall until he could hear the conversation in the kitchen.

"How was your day, honey?" W.J. asked Janice.

"It was good. Was your day good?" Janice asked afraid to say too much.

"It was a great day. I had five service calls today.

Starting my own business was the best thing I could have done. Since tomorrow is Saturday, I'm going to take Joey with me on service calls. I could use his help," W.J. said.

Joey thought about the next day. He had gone on enough service calls in the last four years to know that there were all sorts of mistakes that could bring on abuse. It would drive him insane if he tried to anticipate each possibility, so he refused to worry about it. In this house, you had to deal with one hour at a time.

He continued to listen. His daddy sounded like he was in a good mood, but Joey would never trust that. It was just about a year ago that the night had started out with his daddy in a good mood. Then his mama told his daddy that she was leaving him. After W.J. left the house, his mama packed them all up and drove to Nashville. They stayed several days and even though they got to go to Opryland, the best thing he remembered about that time was the sense of peace and security that overcame him. He knew that his daddy didn't know where they were and there was no way for him to find them. He wondered what the rest of that night might have been like if his mama hadn't packed them up and left. Then they returned home and he found out. That was the night that Joey slept with a knife under his pillow. His daddy had threatened to kill his mama, grandparents, aunt, and uncle. Joey was afraid that if he did try to kill everybody, he wouldn't stop before he came after him and Jason. He stood in the hallway a few minutes longer thinking about that night. He was so scared that he remembered lying there in the dark praying for a long time. Then something happened that he had never experienced before. He felt a hand on his back. He knew the room was empty except for Jason asleep in the other bed. When he felt the hand on his back, he heard the Lord say, "You're going to be okay". Joey had a sense of peace flood over him and he was able to sleep after that.

Slipping back down the hall, Joey knew the Lord would keep His word and that he would be okay. His concern was for the rest of his family.

"Hey, Jason. I think you can come on out. It sounds like he's in a good mood," he whispered as he entered the room.

"I think I'll stay in here and play until dinnertime," Jason said as he pulled out his Matchbox cars and started to play.

Jason wasn't in a hurry to encounter his daddy again. The day before had been enough contact to last him for the rest of his life. He was outside playing in the front yard when W.J. came home from work. Until his daddy stopped the truck and got out in a rage, Jason had forgotten that he left his bicycle in the driveway. His daddy picked the bicycle up and threw it into the yard, got back in the truck and pulled it up the driveway. Jason stood in the yard with his feet feeling like they were anchored to the ground in concrete. He couldn't run. He had tried that once before and the consequences were very painful. W.J. approached him.

"How many times do I have to tell you to keep your bike out of the driveway?!" he screamed.

"I'm sorry, I forgot, please don't hit me," seven-year-old Jason pleaded.

W.J. hit Jason in the head knocking him to the ground and then he pressed his work boot across the child's mouth.

"If you would think more, then you wouldn't have to run your mouth apologizing after you got in trouble," W.J. screamed. He removed his foot from Jason's mouth and stormed into the house.

Jason slowly got up and made his way around to the outside faucet. He washed the dirt off his face, the tears out of his eyes and the blood off his lip. Later he slipped in the house unnoticed and went to his bedroom.

Jason, like Joey, never knew what to expect. His bicycle in the driveway had caused great trouble, but earlier in the week, Joey broke the bathroom window with a baseball. When his daddy got home from work and his mama told him what happened, he just smiled and said he would pick up a new window pane the next day. It never made sense what would make him mad so Jason was perfectly content to stay in his room and play with his toys.

The rest of the evening was uneventful. Joey and Jason watched some television after dinner, and scurried off to bed at the first opportunity. Once you were in bed, you were usually safe for the rest of the evening.

The next day Joey got up as early as he could to be ready for the day. There was no use antagonizing his daddy by making him late for the first service call. They ate breakfast and left immediately.

Janice was concerned for Joey. She knew the kind

of day that might be in store for him. Joey had told her on two different occasions that his daddy had made him help lift a freezer or other large appliance. Being only ten-years-old, he couldn't lift his end. That had resulted in him having his head beat against the freezer until a family friend happened to walk in and put a stop to it.

Joey knew what kind of day was ahead also. He determined in his young mind that he would try to do everything just right so that no beating would happen. As they loaded the truck for the day, W.J. told Joey to put a tank of compressed air in the back. It was all Joey could do to lift the tank high enough to get it in. He was proud of himself for getting the heavy tank loaded like his daddy had told him to do. That should please him. Driving down the road, they turned a sharp curve and the tank rolled out onto the road.

"You didn't tie it down!" W.J. screamed. "You've got to start thinking for yourself. No one is going to think for you," he continued in his rage as he punched Joey in the head several times.

Joey didn't respond. He just tried to deflect the blows with his arms over his head.

The next Saturday Joey had to repeat the same nightmare. He was going with his daddy on service calls. His young stomach stayed in knots continually and good sound sleep was a luxury that he didn't know. He loaded the compressed air tanks, this time remembering to tie them down. He handed his daddy every tool he asked for and he made sure they were the correct ones. The day was going along fairly well.

"Joey, go out and back the truck out of the driveway. Park it in the street, because the owners will be back before we get through. They will need room to park," W.J. instructed a terrified Joey.

"I've never driven the truck, daddy," Joey said.

"Go on, you've watched me enough, you ought to be able to figure it out, just don't hit anything," he said with an edge of anger in his voice.

Joey reluctantly walked outside and crawled up in the driver's seat. He knew that in and up was reverse on the column shift. His legs barely reached the clutch and brake. He figured he probably didn't need to worry about the gas since he wanted to make sure that he didn't go fast enough to hit anything. He started the truck, depressed the clutch and slipped the gear shift into reverse. So far so good. He kept his foot hovering over the brake and started to release the clutch. He was slowly rolling backwards down the driveway when his daddy ran out of the house yelling. Joey immediately hit the brake. He had no idea what he had done wrong, maybe nothing at all, but it didn't matter. W.J. thought he had done something wrong. His daddy reached in through the driver's window, grabbed Joey's head and started beating it against the steering wheel. Somehow Joey managed to turn off the ignition. When W.J. was through 'disciplining' him for whatever mistake he had made, Joey slid across to the passenger seat. He held his aching head as they travelled back home.

The next Saturday, Joey was relieved to find that his daddy didn't want him to go on the service calls. After

Christmas 1973

March 1974

W.J. left the house, Joey and Jason went out in the front yard to play.

"Joey, would you bring me the flashlight from the glove compartment of the car?" Janice called from the front door.

"Sure, Mama," Joey answered as he headed to the family station wagon.

As he got the flashlight out, he saw something interesting in the glove compartment. There was a small bottle of touch up paint for the car. He had never noticed that before and couldn't resist looking at it. He carefully opened it to see what it looked like inside the small bottle. The bottle was so tiny that as he opened it, it slipped out of his hand and hit the front seat between his legs. He grabbed the bottle, but not in time. Paint splattered on the edge of the seat. Joey was terrified. He grabbed the flashlight and ran in the house.

"Mama! Mama!"

"What's the matter?" Janice asked rushing out of the kitchen.

"When I got the flashlight out, I saw this little bottle of paint. I wanted to look inside it so I carefully opened it, but it was so small it slipped out of my hand. I got paint on the car seat. Mama, what can I use to get it off? If daddy sees it, he'll beat me for sure," Joey explained.

"Oh my goodness! Let's go see it," she said as they ran to the car.

Janice panicked as she saw the quarter-size blob of paint on the edge of the passenger seat.

"Get Jason and Julie and get in the back seat!"

she said as she hurried inside for her purse and car keys.

Joey did as he was told and they rushed to a nearby body shop.

"Mr. Byrom, can you get some paint off of the front seat of our car. It's very important that I get it cleaned off. It might not be completely dry yet," Janice explained to the owner of the business.

Mr. Byrom took some cleaner and a rag out to the station wagon. Joey watched anxiously as the man worked and worked on the seat. The paint was slowly coming out. About ten minutes later, you couldn't tell that there had ever been paint even near the seat. Mr. Byrom was so moved by the obvious fear and concern that he was sensing from Janice and Joey, that he gave them a replacement bottle of the touch up paint.

"Thank you so much, Mr. Byrom," Joey said breathing a sigh of relief.

"You're welcome young man, just be sure to leave this bottle in the glove compartment, okay?" he said with a wink.

On the way back home, Janice and Joey silently thanked the Lord for the kindness of a stranger. Mr. Byrom had no idea what he had saved Joey from that night.

A couple of days later, W.J. told Joey to wash the truck. Joey immediately went to gather all the supplies that he needed to do the job. While he was soaping the truck, Julie walked up to him.

"Joey, come play with me," she said looking up at him.

"I can't play right now, Julie. Dad wants me to

wash his truck."

"But I wanna play," Julie said, starting to get upset.

"Julie, go play with Jason before you get me in trouble. I don't want you to get in trouble either. Go on and find Jason, he'll play with you," Joey tried to gently get her to understand. Julie finally went looking for Jason.

Later that day, Joey and Jason were in their rooms wrestling. W.J. was not at home, Janice was outside and had asked the boys to watch their sister. Julie was just watching the boys play but she soon became bored and wandered into the kitchen. Julie loved Sweettarts and spied a bottle with all orange ones in it. She pushed a chair to the kitchen cabinet and climbed up to get the bottle of orange Sweettarts. She ate several, but they didn't taste as good as the last time she had them.

"Julie! What are you doing?" Joey screamed as he entered the kitchen looking for his little sister.

"Eatin' Sweettarts, Joey," Julie said.

He grabbed the bottle of baby aspirin from Julie's hand. He had no idea how many she had eaten. He picked Julie up and ran outside looking for his mama. He found her cleaning out the car.

"Mama! Julie got the baby aspirin and ate some. I don't know how many," he shouted as he rushed up to the car. She rushed her to the bathroom and tried to get her to throw up. She vomited but Janice wasn't sure she got all of the aspirin out. They watched her closely for a while and when she started acting as if she didn't feel well, they determined that she needed to go to the hospital.

"Joey! Jason! Get in the car. We have to take Julie to the emergency room, hurry!" Janice shouted as she grabbed her purse.

At the hospital, they pumped Julie's stomach. She was a very sick little girl and was in danger of losing her life. Joey felt responsible for her eating the aspirin. He had gotten distracted from watching her while wrestling with Jason and he carried the guilt around like a heavy backpack. Even the consolation of Julie improving, didn't lessen the guilt that he felt. Julie stayed in the hospital for several days but made a complete recovery.

The next few months passed with the usual beatings. Joey or Jason would accidently leave a toy laying around or not respond quick enough to a demand by their daddy. He would either take off his leather belt and hit them repeatedly wherever the blows landed, or he would hit them with his fists in the same manner. The entire time that he was beating them, he was yelling in anger.

W.J. acted as if he thought he was disciplining them with his beatings, but Joey knew the difference between beating and discipline. He learned it quite by accident. One day a neighborhood friend mentioned getting a spanking the day before.

"What did you get a spanking for? Did you leave a toy laying out?" Joey asked.

"No, I don't get spankings for things like that. I lied to my mama and told her that I didn't have any homework. My teacher sent a note home to tell my parents that I hadn't been turning in my homework and that I was failing my math class because of it," the friend admitted.

"Wow! You probably deserved a spanking for that. How does your daddy spank you?" Joey asked.

"Well, first of all, he sat me down and explained to me that when we choose to do the wrong thing, there are consequences. Then he told me why lying was wrong and then I got the consequences."

"What were the consequences?"

"My daddy leaned me across his knee and spanked me on my bottom with this little wooden paddle that we have. He gave me five licks for lying. Boy did they hurt!"

Joey thought about this for a long time. He watched this neighborhood friend whenever he was with his daddy. He saw such affection between them. Joey knew that he had never felt affection for, or from, his daddy and he never expected that he would. As he observed his friend, he realized what the difference was between discipline and beating. When you were disciplined, you were lovingly corrected for a genuine mistake. When you were beaten, you were hit repeatedly, in anger, for any little thing that irritated the one doing the beating. Big difference.

One day, Joey and Jason were both with their grandparents, Mr. and Mrs. Quick, when they realized that they weren't the only ones that had reason to fear W.J. Mr. Quick got a phone call from his son to meet him at a certain place in Tullahoma. Mrs. Quick and the boys rode into town with him in the truck. They arrived at the appointed meeting place, and W.J. and his assistant Ralph drove up right after them. What they didn't know at the time was that Ralph had just told him that he was quitting. W.J. had instantly exploded and called his dad to meet him in town.

When W.J. stopped the truck, he jumped out and headed for his father's truck. Ralph sat in the service truck unaware of what was going on. W.J. reached through the passenger window and opened the glove compartment.

"Where's the gun?!" he demanded.

"I took it out of the truck a couple of months ago, why?" Mr. Quick asked him.

W.J. didn't answer. He just turned, got back in his truck and left with Ralph. Joey and Jason knew if the gun had been in their granddad's truck, their daddy would have killed Ralph. The rage was no longer limited to their family.

It was May 1974 and school was nearing an end. Joey had finally spoken his mind to his mama a few days earlier. Driving down the road one day after school, Joey had blurted out, 'Why don't we just divorce daddy?'. He was shocked to hear himself say that. He thought he was just thinking it, but evidently he had said it. It was a load off his mind to let her know how he felt.

Since it was near the end of the school year, his mama, who was a member of the Tullahoma Junior Woman's Club, was obligated to chaperone the Sub-Deb Sorority dance. She picked up dinner for the children and W.J. and headed home.

Janice had decided that she was going to tell W.J. that she wanted a divorce. After being held at gun point on the couch all night the previous week, she had summoned up enough courage to make it official. Earlier that day, Janice had asked W.J. if they could talk, but he didn't have time. As she was dressing to go to the dance, he entered the bedroom and insisted that they talk then. She tried to put him off, but he wouldn't take no for an answer.

"W.J., I don't have time to talk now. I have to chaperone the dance. I'm supposed to be there in thirty minutes," Janice explained as she walked into the kitchen. W.J. started hitting her.

Between blows she screamed, "I want a divorce!"

Joey heard the commotion. He could tell by the tone of W.J.'s voice that this was going to be a rough one.

"Jason, run next door to Mrs. Regina's house and have her call Daddy Joe and Nanny," Joey instructed his terrified brother.

W.J. continued to strike her knocking her to the floor each time. He grabbed her and started dragging her down the hall, stopping to get the deer rifle on the way. She struggled to her feet as he pointed the gun at her.

Joey ran in from the living room and placed himself between the barrel of the rifle and his mama.

"Please don't kill Mama," was all he said.

W.J. lowered the rifle. The police and the Hamptons arrived soon afterwards. After recording the information of what happened, the police informed Janice that she could leave the home, but she could not take the children with her. Her parents were extremely concerned for her physical condition and they insisted she come to their house. W.J. promised the police that he would put the gun away and that he wouldn't harm the children.

On the way to the Hampton's house, they stopped by the police department hoping to put an end to this nightmare.

"I need to swear out a warrant for my husband's arrest," Janice said as she limped to the counter, the evidence of the beating she had gotten was obvious.

"Oh, now, you know you don't want to do that," the officer in charge said. "Why don't you just go home and sleep on it?"

This was impossible! Janice left again without filing a complaint. So she went to the Hampton's house and phoned a respected Tullahoma attorney.

"I need help. My name is Janice Quick and my husband has just severely beaten me. It's been going on for twelve years and I need to get myself and my three children out of this abusive environment," Janice told the attorney.

"I'm sorry Mrs. Quick, but my schedule is full. If you will come to my office in the morning at 11 a.m., I'll have one of my partners meet with you."

"Thank you," she said.

Janice hung up the phone and it immediately rang. Joe answered it.

"Joe, I'm coming over there to give y'all something," W.J. said and hung up.

"Well, W.J. is coming over here to give us something. Who knows what that means?!" Joe told Wilma and Janice.

"I'm going to call Regina and ask her to run next door and check on the kids when W.J. leaves," Janice said as she dialed the phone again.

After the police left their home, Joey, Jason, and Julie went to the boys' bedroom. Joey saw how his mama looked when she left and he was very worried about her. She was hurt badly and he didn't know if she would get the help that she needed. There was nothing he could do to help her, but he was determined to take care of his brother and sister.

He stood inside the bedroom door listening for any activity from his daddy. He heard nothing but silence on the other side.

"Jason, help me push our beds together and we can all sleep in here tonight," Joey said.

"I wanna sweep in my bed," Julie protested.

"But this will be fun. It will be like a campout," Joey convinced her.

They all climbed into the two twin beds that were now side by side and tried to settle down for the night. A few minutes later, Joey heard the front door open and close, then he heard his daddy pull out of the driveway. Being left alone wasn't nearly as scary as being left in the house with him. Joey felt himself relax. Then he heard a knock on the door. He knew it couldn't be his daddy, since he had just heard him leave. He got up, ran to the door, and opened it. It was Mrs. Regina.

"Hi, Mrs. Regina," Joey said stepping to the side to let her in.

"Joey, are you, Jason and Julie okay?" she asked.

"Yes ma'am, we're fine. Come see what we did," Joey said as he led her down the hallway.

When Regina saw the bedroom with the twin beds pushed together, she was touched at how the two boys were watching over their sister.

"Your mom won't be back tonight, but she asked me to run over here and make sure you were safe. Are you going to be okay?" Regina asked.

"Yes ma'am, we'll be fine," Joey assured her.

*****

Joe watched out the window for W.J. to pull into the driveway. He wanted to keep him out of the house in case this went downhill. Within ten minutes, Joe saw the familiar lights of W.J.'s work truck turning into the driveway. He slipped out the door and walked up to the car. W.J. handed the deer rifle out the window to Joe, backed out of the driveway and drove off.

The next morning W.J. called the Hamptons to tell Janice that she could come for the children, so she and her parents immediately drove across town and got them. Because of the severity of the beating, after she returned to her parents house and she knew the children were safe, she went to the doctor. She had blood in her ear accompanied by numerous cuts and bruises from the many blows she received from his fists. While she was at the doctors office, W.J. showed up. He insisted on taking her prescriptions to the drug store to have them filled. His remorseful acts of kindness were nothing new to Janice. She knew they were nothing but another ploy to get her to return, but this time, it didn't work. Later that day, Janice filed for divorce.

Chapter 7

Distant Thunder

The divorce was filed for on June 18, 1974. Janice and the children remained in their home, but W.J. moved out. She stood firm on her decision to remove herself and the children from W.J.'s abuse. But, during this time she also attempted to help W.J. as he sought medical assistance. He went to a local physician about his nerves and then began to see a psychiatrist in Murfreesboro. His one request was that Janice and Joe accompany him on the forty-minute drive to Murfreesboro for his psychiatric appointments. Before the first session, Janice and Wilma planned to drive W.J. to his parents' house in Estill Springs, because he needed to pick up some clean clothes.

"Wilma, I'm very concerned about what you might say to my mama," W.J. said anxiously, sitting in the car holding his Bible.

"W.J., I would never say anything bad to your mama, but if it will make you feel better, I won't talk at all," Wilma offered.

"I can't believe you! You're a Christian and you

won't even talk to my mama!" W.J. accused her. Before they got to his parents home, he jumped out of the car and took off running.

Not knowing what he was thinking or what he might do, Janice turned the car around and returned to her parents' house.

A few hours later, Joe was driving home from work to get ready for the trip to Murfreesboro when he passed W.J. walking down the road holding his Bible. Joe picked him up and continued to the house. The four of them drove to his psychiatric appointment.

"I want to be admitted to the hospital," W.J. demanded when they arrived at the doctor's office.

The doctor's office sent him to the hospital admitting clerk.

"I'm having trouble talking so I would like for Janice to answer the questions for me," he told the clerk at the hospital as he masterfully manipulated the situation. The clerk asked Janice all the standard medical questions. Then she started the personal section of the admittance papers.

"What is his religious affiliation?" the clerk asked Janice.

"Methodist," she answered. W.J. had always said that he was a Methodist even though he had been attending the Baptist church with her since their marriage.

"NO! I'm Baptist. I want a vasectomy!" he screamed.

Janice and her parents stood there in shock listening to his insane ravings. They had no idea if he was truly disturbed or if his behavior was an Oscar winning performance.

He continued his trips to the psychiatrist in Murfreesboro and also was treated by his local physician. The local doctor confided in Janice that he thought W.J. was suicidal. They decided to consult a local minister together.

"Janice, are you telling me that W.J. has abused and beaten you for the twelve years you've been married and he's also been abusing the children?" The minister asked in shock. He had known W.J. for years, but had never seen his true nature. W.J. always presented himself as such a decent, law-abiding, and upstanding citizen, that, basically, the whole world was fooled.

"Yes sir, that's what I'm telling you," she answered.

"W.J., is Janice's account of your married life accurate?" He asked.

"Yes, it's accurate."

"W.J., what kind of a wife and mother would you say that Janice is?"

"Good," was all he said.

After a little more discussion, the minister agreed with Janice that divorce might be the correct choice.

"WHAT?! How can you agree with her? I thought divorce was against your belief! What kind of preacher are you to agree to break up a marriage?!" W.J. went into a rage.

"Now, you hold on there a minute! I'll not have you acting like that in here. Janice, go on and leave," the minister said as Janice scurried out. He had a small taste of the rage and anger that Janice had dealt with for twelve long years. He detained W.J. long enough for Janice to get away safely.

As she suspected, Janice met a lot of resistance to divorcing W.J. Even his own mother begged her to stay with him. One day Janice drove to Mrs. Quick's to pick up the children. She went inside and W.J. was there. Mrs. Quick tried to convince Janice that staying in her marriage was the right thing to do, based on the fact that she had never left her husband. Janice always had a good relationship with her mother-in-law, but she held her ground this time. She told Mrs. Quick that she would not endure the beatings any longer and that she would not have Joey and Jason living with the brutality. They were young enough to learn a different way of life.

Mrs. Quick and W.J. both got up from their chairs and approached Janice on the couch. They knelt down on the floor on either side of Janice and started begging.

"Janice, think of the children. I never left my husband because of the children," Mrs. Quick said.

"Yeah, and just look what you raised!" Janice said.

W.J. and his mother both gasped and fell back. Janice got up, walked right between them and left the house. As she walked to the car, she was stunned at what had come out of her mouth. She never intended to say that, it just happened, but it felt good.

W.J. appealed to a number of people in the community to plead his case with Janice. All of these people saw the 'good' side of him that was presented in public. They had never been on the receiving end of his anger or maybe their responses would have been different. A local hospital administrator called Janice several times urging her to return to her husband. Also, a community psychologist who specialized in marriage and family relationships, told Janice "I don't think he'll ever hurt you again". W.J. also started receiving help from the mental health facility in Tullahoma. He was on several medications prescribed from there. All this was to show Janice that he was making every effort to get help and learn to control himself. She remained unconvinced.

During this time, W.J. did a lot of appliance repair work for the local hospital. Janice had to be at the hospital one day and ran into the administrator. He asked her to come into his office. She had no sooner sat down than he began badgering her about the divorce.

"Janice, please don't divorce W.J. He's a good man. I'm sure he will change," he coerced her.

"I'm not calling the divorce off, but I will have to start looking for a job," she stated.

"Well, why don't you put the divorce off until the first of the year. After January, I can offer you a job in the hospital pharmacy," he suggested.

"I'm not postponing the divorce, but I would be interested in the pharmacy job," she said.

During the months before the divorce was granted, W.J. continued to plead with Janice. He would call her at home or show up at the Hamptons' when he saw her car there. One day when he caught her at her parents' house, she saw him coming and met him at the door.

"What do you want?" she asked, frustrated at the

whole situation.

"I just wanted you to know that I'm going to kill myself," W.J. informed her.

"You need to leave," Janice said.

"I'm going to kill myself," he stated again.

This went on until Janice got mad. She closed the door and went to the phone to call her lawyer.

"Nelson, W.J. is outside my parents' house and won't leave. All he keeps saying is that he's going to kill himself," she explained.

"I've got a few minutes so I'll call his lawyer and see if he won't meet me over there. We'll see if we can talk some sense into him. Don't let him in the house," Nelson instructed.

"You don't have to worry about that!" Janice told him.

The lawyers drove up at the same time and found W.J. standing in the driveway. Janice had the door open and he was insisting that he was going to kill himself.

"W.J., let's go somewhere and talk about this," W.J.'s lawyer said.

"No need to talk about it. My mind's made up."

Janice couldn't stand this charade any longer. She knew that he was just bluffing to try to get her to call off the divorce.

"Go ahead," she said. "I'll do your funeral up right. I'll even get you a first class casket, and I'll ask Miriam to sing your favorite song!"

The lawyers were shocked at how she handled the situation, but something was working, because W.J.

walked off muttering, "No judge is going to tell me if my marriage is valid, or when I can see my kids, or how much I have to pay for their upkeep." He got in his car and left.

"Does this go on all the time?" W.J.'s lawyer asked Janice.

"He comes by every so often to threaten me or himself. I've gotten used to his bluffs. I wouldn't have called y'all this time except he wouldn't leave."

"Call me anytime," Nelson said as they each returned to their cars.

W.J.'s many attempts to stop the divorce didn't work. As a last ditch effort, he got himself admitted to the hospital the day before the scheduled court date with a 'No Visitors' sign posted on the door. Both attorneys talked it over and approached W.J. He finally agreed to the divorce. The property settlement would be worked out at a later date.

Janice and Joe had to appear before the judge to give their testimony of grounds for the divorce. Joe took the stand and told of the repeated abuse that his daughter and grandchildren had suffered. Then it was Janice's turn to speak.

"I don't care if you don't give me the divorce, I'm not going back to him," was the first thing out of Janice's mouth when she took the stand. There had not been a single man in governmental authority that had believed her yet, and she thought that the judge wouldn't be any different.

"Janice, just calm down and tell the judge what your life was like with W.J.," her attorney instructed her.

"My life with W.J. has been one beating after another. I've put up with this for twelve years and I've had enough," she said.

"What caused you to 'have enough'?" The judge asked her.

"A few months ago, he made me sit on the couch all night with a rifle pointed at me. He told me if I so much as breathed hard, he was going to kill me. That's when I had enough," Janice stated.

The gavel hit the desktop hard. "Divorce granted!" said the judge.

The divorce was granted in July, but would not be final for sixty days. During the sixty days, someone tipped the police off that W.J. was riding around town with a loaded shotgun. The police started patrolling around town looking for W.J. Unaware of the situation, and with the boys safely with Wilma and Joe, Janice and Julie went to Kay's house for a visit. During the time they were there, Kenneth decided to go for a late evening walk. It was a beautiful day and a walk was the perfect way to unwind. He was just a few blocks from the house when W.J. pulled up to the curb and got out of the truck. He was carrying a shotgun. Kenneth didn't wait to see what he wanted, he just started running as fast as he could. He had seen that crazed look on W.J.'s face before and he didn't want to know what was next. Before he stopped, he realized he was over a mile away near the local high school. He was not even sure how he got away and lost W.J. He ducked into a phone booth and called a family friend to pick him up. He stayed hidden in the phone booth until the friend arrived.

At the same time that Kenneth was running for his life, the police arrived at Kay's house.

"Mrs. Quick, we need all of you to come with us. Mr. Quick is in town with a loaded shotgun and we are setting up road blocks to hopefully find him," the police officer informed them.

"Where are you taking us?" Janice asked.

"We are taking you, your sister, and your children to your parents house. We want all of you to stay together there," he answered.

"Where's Kenneth?" Kay asked.

"I haven't seen him," replied the officer.

Janice, Julie, Kay, Kim, and Jada rode in the back seat of the police car to Wilma and Joe's house.

"I'm worried about Kenneth," Kay told the officer when she got out of the car. "He went for a walk about forty five minutes ago. He should have been back by now."

"We will cruise the neighborhood around your house to see if we can find him," he assured her.

A short time later, they were relieved to see Kenneth walking through the door. He told them about his terrifying encounter with W.J. The police continued the roadblocks but never apprehended him. They searched the town for him and finally found him in the last place they would have expected. He had returned to work and was in his appliance store. He had disassembled the gun and hidden parts of it in a number of different appliances. He was not arrested.

The following day, Janice's attorney petitioned the judge for an injunction to keep W.J. away from her and her family. He wasn't allowed to call her or to step foot on their property. However, a restraining order wouldn't protect them completely. W.J. had visitation rights every Thursday for four hours and every other weekend. He picked the children up at the Hampton's house, but Janice was having to force the children to comply with the court order. At one point, the attorney met with the children to explain that Janice was making them go to their dad's because she would face serious charges if she didn't. It might have explained it to them, but it didn't make it any easier. Joey and Jason were very resentful about it and Julie cried every time she was sent with W.J.

All summer long, Janice had been working closely with W.J.'s secretary. Mrs. Ray was a sweet lady in her early 70s, and whenever W.J. was out on a service call, Mrs. Ray ran the appliance store. She also took care of all the paperwork, except for the financial bookwork. Janice had always taken care of the financial end of the business, but the time had come to train someone else. Mrs. Ray was the obvious choice so they talked on the phone frequently. As the final divorce decree was nearing, Mrs. Ray became nervous.

"Janice, please don't come back to him. He's too dangerous. I've been worried all summer that you would change your mind and try to patch things up between the two of you," Mrs. Ray confided in Janice in late August.

"You don't have to worry about that! I'll never go back to him. I'm happier, the kids are happier, and we are definitely safer," Janice answered.

"Everybody is happier, except W.J. You wouldn't believe the amount of pill bottles that he has. I've never seen so much medicine. I'm afraid that I'll come in here one morning and find him dead on the floor."

"Oh goodness! Mrs. Ray, I didn't know he was taking so much medicine. Just try to keep an eye on him, but for heaven's sake, don't let him know that you are worried about him. He might lose his temper, and believe you me, you don't want to see that!" Janice told her.

September came and so did the final divorce papers. Twelve years to the month since their marriage began, it ended. But W.J. wouldn't give up. He continued to telephone Janice to beg her to return. One day he would say, "Come back to me...Let's make the marriage work," and the next day he would tell her, "If you really leave me, there is nothing to live for...I'll kill myself!"

As October slipped by, it was time for the last step, the property settlement agreement. Janice went to W.J.'s attorney's office to sign the documents.

"Steve, I have a doctor's appointment. I think I have strep throat, so I need to come back later to sign the papers," Janice explained to the attorney.

"That's fine, Janice. Just come back when you get out of the doctor's office, if you feel up to it," he answered.

After her appointment, Janice decided to go back to the lawyer's office and finish this nightmare. As she entered the lobby, the attorney's secretary asked her to wait and she would check with him. When the secretary called him, he came out of his office immediately.

"Janice, where are the kids?" W.J.'s attorney asked her.

"They are at Kay's, why?"

"You need to leave here, go get the kids, and go straight to your parents' home," the attorney told her. "W.J. is in my office and he's acting very irrational. He keeps saying that he's going to kill himself. I've told him if he plans to do that, then we need to get a will made up and put on file, but he's not in any state to do that right now. You can come back tomorrow and sign the papers. Please leave and be careful."

Janice left immediately, picked up the kids, and went to her parents' home.

Fear was still Janice's constant companion. She was living in their house but always kept extra clothes and personal items in the car in case they had to stay at her sister's or parents' house. There were several times that they did leave the house at night, due to W.J.'s threats.

In early December, Janice visited her sister-in-law in the hospital. Mrs. Quick, W.J.'s mother, was there so they discussed their plans for Christmas.

"W.J. told me that he planned to buy tape recorders for the children for Christmas," Mrs. Quick remarked.

"Oh no! I just bought tape recorders for Joey and Jason. I need to tell him before he spends his money on something they already have. I'll stop by the appliance store and tell him on my way home," Janice told them.

Janice began to pray on the way to the appliance

store, "Lord, if I'm supposed to stop, then please let his truck be there," and it was.

When she entered the store, W.J. was with a customer so she stood at the front of the store waiting for him to finish his sale.

"You can wait on that lady while I look around if you want to," the customer suggested.

"Oh, that's my ex-wife, she probably just wants more money," he told the customer.

Janice was stunned. It was very out of character for him to make derogatory comments in front of customers, or anyone else for that matter. She stayed and waited for him to finish with the customer before she spoke.

"W.J., your mother just told me that you wanted to buy tape recorders for the children for Christmas. I already bought them so I wanted to let you know before you....", she trailed off as she saw the look in his eyes. It frightened her. It was a vacant, terrifying look that reflected much more than just anger. Janice quickly ran to her car. At first, W.J. tried to hold onto the car door to keep her from leaving, but after she got into the car and started the engine, he started yanking at the door. As she pulled away, he kicked the car. Janice was so terrified that she backed out onto a busy highway without even looking.

There was very little communication between them for the next two weeks. His visitations with the children continued, but that was the only contact they had. Despite all of this, Janice and the children were trying their best to enjoy the holiday season. They were involved in many activities at their church, and Joey, 11, Jason, 8, and Julie, 3, all had parts in the Sunday night Christmas program.

Chapter 8

It was December 22, 1974 and everybody was excited. It was the Christmas program day. The children could hardly sit still in the church service that morning. Sunday School was loud and rowdy with the teachers trying to get in a last minute practice for all the speeches and the play that would be performed that night. The Christmas program was such a special time for all the children involved. Everybody wore their best clothes, the lights were turned down low, and it was their time to shine. All the children under nine years old had speeches to recite to the congregation. The older children were all in the Christmas play.

The large cedar Christmas tree stood in the corner on Sunday morning already decorated with all sorts of ornaments, although the lights wouldn't be turned on until right before the program that night. Some of the teenagers had met on Saturday to prepare bags of candy and fruit to be given to everyone in attendance. All the Sunday school classes drew names for gift giving and, of course, the teachers and students all had gifts for each other. As everyone arrived on Sunday night, they placed their gifts under the tree. The anticipation of the evening was almost unbearable.

Joey, Jason, and Julie were just as excited as all the other children. The past few months had been the happiest they had ever known. Even when they had to spend time with their daddy on Thursday evenings and on weekends, he wasn't abusing them. Of course, they didn't know how long that would last, so there was always fear associated with staying with him. But they wouldn't think about that today, because it was the day of the Christmas program. Presents tonight, presents on Christmas Eve with family, and presents from Santa on Christmas morning. It was going to be a great week.

When the morning service was over, Janice and the kids went home for lunch. Afterward, she rolled Julie's hair while the boys spent the afternoon playing. They were too excited to rest for the big night. The program started at 7 p.m. so Janice fixed their dinner around 5 p.m. After dinner, Julie asked if she could call W.J. to make sure he was coming to the program. She had a short speech and wanted to make sure that her daddy heard her. Joey and Jason had already told him about the program, but Julie was insistent about telephoning him. Janice helped her call him and afterward Janice spoke to him requesting that he come for the children's sake. He started arguing with her. About thirty minutes after she hung up from talking with W.J., the phone rang and it was W.J.'s father.

"Janice, W.J.'s on his way into town and you need to be careful," Mr. Quick warned her.

"Mr. Quick, why would you think it was necessary to warn me about him now? He's not as bad as he was when we were still married," she told him.

"Janice, he's been lying on the bed all day just staring at the ceiling. A little while ago, he got up and left. He's in a bad way. You need to go straight to your parents' house," he explained. "Please be careful."

If Mr. Quick was worried enough to call her, it must be serious. Janice immediately dressed the children and called her parents.

"Mama, Mr. Quick just called me to let me know that W.J. was acting strangely and, as he put it, was 'in a bad way'. He said that W.J. had just left his house," Janice told Wilma.

"You need to come on over here. He wouldn't dare bother you at our house."

"I'm leaving as soon as I get the children's coats. Please tell Daddy what Mr. Quick told me," Janice said.

Janice and the children got to the Hampton's around 5:45 p.m. Kay, Kenneth, and their two girls were there, and a few other church friends were just leaving. Everyone was excited and talking about the Christmas program, when W.J. pulled into the driveway. Rather than have him come into the house, they all stepped outside. W.J. was in a belligerent mood. He started yelling and arguing with everybody. Janice had highlighted her hair and he was even screaming about that. Joe, who was suffering from pneumonia, had also stepped outside. He heard all he wanted and slipped back into the house to call the police.

When Joe returned he informed W.J. that the police were on their way. W.J. returned to his truck, still mouthing, and left the driveway.

"Now that he's gone, we are going to drive on over to the church," Kenneth told them as he and his family left.

Wilma, Janice, and the children got into Wilma's car. She was driving with Julie and Janice in the front seat, and Joey and Jason in the back seat.

One block away from their house, they saw W.J. pulled over by the police on a side street. He was not detained and his truck was not searched.

"Oh, no, we forgot Julie's doll for her speech. I left it on the couch. We've got to go back and get it," Janice said. So Wilma turned the car around and went back to get the doll. After they left the driveway the second time, they passed the street where W.J. was stopped by the policemen, and he pulled in behind them. Two blocks further down, they passed an intersection. There were two police cars sitting on either side of the intersection facing toward the road Wilma was traveling. Janice saw the police cars and waved frantically, pointing behind them at W.J.'s truck, trying desperately to get their attention. They didn't respond. Right after they passed the police car, W.J. caught up to them.

"Daddy's behind us and there's a gun on the dashboard," Joey yelled.

Just two blocks away from the church, W.J. rammed the back of the car that Wilma was driving.

"Mama, drive to the police station!" Janice

screamed.

"Yeah, Nanny, go to the police station," Joey and Jason pleaded.

"He never acts up in a crowd. If we can just get to the church parking lot, he will leave us alone," Wilma said as she turned off of the road into the parking lot. She drove to an empty space at the end of the Sunday School wing and parked the car. W.J. pulled up directly behind them. Sensing that something was not right, Joey jumped out of the car on the passenger side and ran into the back door of the church to get help. Wilma saw a visiting couple walking towards the building a few cars away, so she quickly rolled her window down.

"Ma'am, please go get help," Wilma said to the woman who glanced over at her.

"He's going to kill us," Janice shouted out the window.

The woman continued to walk towards the front of the church. Janice had no idea if she believed them or had even heard them.

Kay and her family were outside the front of the church talking. She looked up and saw W.J.'s truck as she entered.

"Well, he's here," she said, with her usual disgust for W.J.

It was 6:42 and most of the people were already in the church preparing for the program. However, a few people were still arriving, parking their cars and walking up to the church. With no concern about who was around, W.J. walked straight to the driver's side door and shot

Wilma. Janice was calling out to her mother. Julie, who was in the seat between them, was crying, and Wilma had slumped over the steering wheel. The bullet had hit her in the left arm and ricocheted through the windshield. Before Janice could get out, W.J. was at her door.

"Cover Julie up," he ordered her.

Janice threw Julie down on the seat of the car and fell across her. Immediately, Janice's head started hurting. She couldn't understand why, unless W.J. had hit her in the head with his gun. She felt herself slumping down further into the seat. As she did, she heard her mother scream. *Thank God she's alive,* Janice thought. Then she heard another shot to her left. W.J. had shot her mother a second time.

Joey entered the back door and ran through the church looking for help. Many of the adults noticed him running, but he never said a word until he reached the front porch. A lot of the men were standing out front talking and greeting people who were entering the church.

Joey ran through the crowd screaming, "He's got a gun and he's killing everybody!" Before the men could react, Joey ran back out to the car. His daddy was standing on the passenger side next to Janice's door. Joey ran around the front of the car and stood face to face with W.J..

"Please, daddy, don't do this!" Joey begged.

"Get out of here! Get away!" W.J. screamed in rage at Joey.

Joey ran back towards the front of the church. Before he could turn the corner, he heard another shot. W.J.

had reached through the window and pulled Janice up by her hair. Putting his gun to the back of her neck he pulled the trigger. She slumped to the floorboard.

It took a few seconds for the men of the church to understand what Joey was saying. He had run off so fast that they were still processing what they had heard. They weren't paying much attention since kids were always running around shouting back and forth between themselves. But there was no other kid with Joey that he might have been playing with. They had heard what they thought were fireworks a few seconds earlier. It was Christmas time and people always shot fireworks at holidays. Then they heard what was definitely a gunshot. Several of them started around the end of the church, when they heard two more gunshots. W.J. fell to the pavement next to the passenger door. All of the shootings had occurred in a matter of seconds.

Jason had remained in the back seat of the car the entire time. He was sitting on the driver's side when W.J. fell to the ground. He opened his door and ran to the front of the church. He passed all the men that were running toward the car.

Jason ran into the church screaming, "Daddy's shooting everybody!"

His Sunday school teacher tried to catch him to calm him down, but in his trauma and pain, he kicked her in the shin.

"Jason, calm down, calm down," she said, unaware of what the child had just witnessed. She hugged him close to comfort him from his obvious fear, but he was inconsolable.

The pain in Janice's head was excruciating. Random thoughts were racing through her head. *Was this how the Kennedy brothers felt when they were shot?* Then she realized she was still alive because she was thinking. Julie was screaming and Janice reached out toward her. As she tried to extend her arms, she felt all feeling leave her body.

"I'm paralyzed," she whispered to herself.

Julie wiggled her legs out from under Janice.

"I want to go inside," Julie said as she crawled over Janice and looked out the window.

"It's okay, Mama, Daddy's asleep now," Julie said.

Kenneth was one of the men on the front porch and he came running up to the car.

"Nanny!" he screamed, calling Wilma by her nickname, not knowing what he was about to find.

He reached in the window to feel for a pulse in Wilma's neck.

"Is she alive?" Janice asked from the darkness.

"Yes. Janice, where are you?" Kenneth asked.

"I'm in the floorboard and I can't move," Janice answered.

Kenneth saw Julie in the front seat.

"Come here, Julie," he said to the three year old. She hesitated in confusion, but then crawled over Wilma and Kenneth took her out of the car.

"W.J. is on my side of the car and I think he's dead," Janice told him.

"Someone has gone for help. Just hang on Janice.

I hear sirens coming so the ambulance should be here soon," Kenneth said.

One of the men from the front porch left to go get Joe. By the time they returned to the church, an ambulance was in the parking lot. Wilma, who was still alive, was removed from the car first. She was attended by the paramedics while they attempted to remove Janice. The door was jammed and they had to bring her through the window. When they got Janice and Wilma in the ambulance, they put W.J. on a stretcher and started to put him on the floor between Wilma and Janice.

"NO! Don't you put him in there with my mama and sister," Kay screamed as she tried to get to the ambulance. Her husband held her back as they closed the doors and sped off to the local hospital. She was understandably hysterical. They had placed the victims and the shooter in the same ambulance. *Didn't they know what that man had taken from her?*

"Get me to the hospital!" she shouted, as the sound of the siren faded.

Kenneth left his two children with a friend at the church and drove Kay, Joe, and Joey to the hospital.

Wilma was unconscious as they raced to the hospital four miles away. Janice was very much conscious and overwhelmed with the chaos. When they arrived, the hospital was buzzing like a hornet's nest due to the nature of the event. Nothing like this had ever happened in this small town. She lay on a stretcher between her mama and her ex-husband and watched as the nurse pulled the sheet over W.J. He was dead.

Kenneth, Kay, Joe, and Joey arrived at the hospital. They informed them that W.J. was dead and that Wilma and Janice were in serious condition.

"I want to see him," Joey stated.

They all looked at the eleven-year-old stunned. Why would he want to see him?

"I want to see him!" Joey repeated to the paramedic that had been with them at the church. The paramedic sat down and pulled Joey over to him.

"Young man, there is no reason for you to see your dad like that. It wouldn't do you any good," he tried to reason with Joey.

"I want to know that he is dead," Joey said emotionless.

"Oh, I see. Well, I can assure you that he is dead. He will not be hurting anyone else ever again," the paramedic assured him. That seemed to satisfy Joey.

After initial x-rays, the medical staff in charge knew that Wilma and Janice needed help far beyond the ability of a small hospital. The specialized equipment and specific expertise needed for head injuries was only available in Nashville. They were quickly transported to Baptist Hospital.

As they removed them from the ambulance in Nashville, Janice was stunned even further to realize that word of W.J.'s actions had reached the media. Lights were blaring and television cameras were rolling as they rushed them into the hospital.

Chapter 9

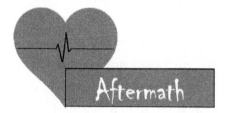

It was early in the morning on December 23rd before Janice got the word that Wilma was going to live. She had survived the six-hour surgery to remove the bullet. The first bullet had struck her left arm but caused no permanent damage. The second bullet entered at her left breast and traveled downward through the stomach and kidney and lodged in her spleen. It had missed her heart by the thickness of a sheet of paper. Wilma was placed in intensive care. Janice, who was also in intensive care, was on heavy medication due to severe headaches, and was drifting in and out of consciousness. They were monitoring her condition to determine when she was stable enough for surgery.

Joey had stayed at the hospital all night with Kay and Kenneth. They had called home that morning to see how Jason and Julie were doing, and were told what the funeral arrangements were.

"Daddy's funeral is tomorrow, Christmas Eve," Joey told Janice. "I don't want to go. Do I have to go to the funeral?"

"No, you don't have to go, but I think you should. If you don't, I'm worried that one day in the future, you will regret not going," she explained.

Because of years of abuse, Joey was so conditioned to do whatever was expected of him that he didn't argue anymore. He and Jason would go to the funeral.

A family friend took Joey back to Tullahoma so that he could sleep. He went to his great-aunt and uncle's house. There were no other children at their house so Joey had the opportunity to rest.

The night before, Jason and Julie had stayed at the church after the ambulance left. The church had a time of intense prayer for Janice and Wilma, then they quickly handed out the gifts and goodie bags to the children and closed the service.

Jason and Julie went home with Janice's cousin, Corrine. Jason had been at her house on several occasions and was comfortable there. Her son Eric was just one year older than Joey and the three of them played together occasionally. The next morning Harold, Corrine's brother, came to break the news to Jason that his dad was dead. Harold took Jason into a bedroom to talk in private.

"Jason, I wanted you to know that your mama and Nanny are in the hospital in Nashville. Nanny had surgery last night and is doing pretty good. Your mama can't have surgery until she's a little stronger, maybe in the next day or two. But I have something very sad to tell you. Your daddy didn't make it, he died," Harold said as gently as he could.

"Okay," Jason replied and turned to walk back into the living room to play with Eric and Laurie, Harold's daughter.

"What's going on?" Eric asked.

"My daddy's dead," Jason replied totally unmoved by the fact.

No one understood Jason and Joey's response to the fact that their dad was gone. But then again, no one understood, or even knew, the torment they had endured at his hands. If there was an emotion there at all, it was something akin to relief.

On Christmas Eve day, Janice's doctor came by her room.

"Would you like to spend Christmas Eve in the operating room with me?" he asked her, trying to lighten the mood.

"If that's the way you want to spend your Christmas Eve, I guess I'm ready to face surgery," Janice responded. After the doctor left the room, she slipped back into unconsciousness again as she waited for them to come get her for surgery.

Many people had been praying for Janice and Wilma for the last two days, their church friends, family, school friends, acquaintances and the town as a whole. This was a major incident in the life of a small town like Tullahoma. Everybody knew somebody that knew somebody that was related to just about anybody in town. But there was no one praying harder than Joe. The past forty-eight hours had taken a toll on him. He split his time between two intensive care units feeling helpless, looking at his wife and his oldest daughter, and all he could do was pray. It didn't feel like enough. If only it hadn't come to this.

Later, as they prepared Janice for surgery, Joey, Jason, and Julie were preparing to attend their dad's funeral. It was being held in a nearby town and the hospital administrator and a family friend would take them.

They were traveling down the road toward the funeral when Richard, the hospital administrator, pulled the car off the road.

"Okay kids, we're going to do this a little differently. Get out of the car," he said. Joey, Jason, and Richard's son got out of the car. Richard opened the trunk and told them to crawl in. They would ride the rest of the way to the funeral in the trunk. Julie remained in the front of the car.

Joey and Jason did as they were told. Richard's son also crawled in the trunk. They had no idea why he was making them ride that way. Joey thought about it all the way to the funeral home. *Were all adults crazy? Why would he do this? Maybe he didn't want the Quicks to know who we were riding with,* Joey thought as he lay there in the darkness. They were only five miles from the funeral home, and that wasn't near enough time for him to figure out why adults do the things that they do.

There were a lot of people at the funeral home and Joey, Jason, and Julie were very uncomfortable being in this crowd. Everyone was pitying them and wanting to hug them. Some were relatives, but most were people they had never met before. The two men that drove them there took them to their seats as the service began. It was extremely difficult to see W.J. in his casket, especially for Julie. She couldn't understand why her daddy was lying up there in front of all these people in his best suit.

"We are here today," the minister said, "to pay tribute to an honorable man. W.J. Quick was well loved by all his friends and family. He was a good provider and husband to Janice, his wife. He was a kind and gentle father to his children, Joey, 11; Jason, 8; and Julie, 3."

Joey was starting to feel sick at his stomach. *Was this man talking about his daddy? These people actually thought he was a good daddy*. He didn't think that he could stand much more of these lies.

"He was a good godly example of a father to his children," he continued.

That did it. Joey jumped up and ran out of the funeral. He couldn't handle hearing such praise for the man who had beaten him, Jason, and their mother for many years. Praise for the man who had just shot his mother and grandmother. Praise for the man that none of these people really knew.

He waited at the car until the two men that brought them returned with Jason and Julie to leave.

"Joey, that was very rude," Richard scolded him. "You should never run out of a funeral. It's very disrespectful of the person who died."

"Not as disrespectful as him beating us for years. That preacher didn't even know anything about my daddy," Joey said as he crawled back in the trunk for the return trip. *None of these people understood. They were here paying respect to the man that had ruined his life. Didn't they know that while they were there lying about how good a man his dad was, his mama and nanny were still fighting for their lives because of him? Didn't that mean anything to them?* Lying in the dark trunk, Joey swallowed the lump in his throat as he thought about his mama in the operating room.

When the surgical team came to get Janice, the surgeon came with them. They had 8-10 people in the room to move her from the bed to the gurney. They were extremely careful not to let her body move in any way. They wanted her to remain straight as a board to avoid any more damage. The surgeon walked with her all the way to the operating room. On the way down the hall, Janice's nose started itching. She was twitching it to get it to stop.

"Janice, is your nose itching?" the surgeon asked her.

"Yes sir, it is," she replied.

He promptly told them to stop pushing her and he reached down and scratched her nose. Once they entered the operating room, they flipped her over onto the operating table with the same slow deliberate movements. She had to have the surgery face down to give them access to her neck. There was a hole in the table for her face to fit in, so all she could see was the operating room floor underneath her.

Before they sedated her for the surgery she heard someone say, "Scissors!"

The next thing she saw was red hair falling onto

the floor around the table.

"Shears!" the voice called for again.

More red hair hit the floor. Janice was almost sick to her stomach. She had worked for months to get her hair down to her shoulders and she had just paid a lot of money to have it highlighted. She wasn't sure if she passed out or if they sedated her, but everything turned black.

The surgery progressed slowly. The bullet that was lodged in Janice's head was removed and the nerves in her neck were repaired. The second bullet had severed her spinal column and was left lodged in a neck muscle. It would do unnecessary damage to remove it, so they decided to leave it where it was.

At the end of the surgery, the surgeon said, "She should be coming around soon."

"I am and IT HURTS!" Janice said, to the surprise of all in the operating room as she slightly moved her left arm. She was only conscious long enough to realize that she was in incredible pain and then she blacked out again. They moved Janice to recovery and started pain medication.

The surgeon approached an exhausted Joe, Kay, and Kenneth. They jumped up when they saw him coming, unsure of what they were about to hear.

"She's doing fine," the surgeon assured them. "At this point, she is paralyzed and the nerves to her left arm are completely severed. However, we trimmed the end of the nerves and cleaned them up. There is a slim possibility that some of them could regenerate and she might regain very basic use of her arm. As a matter of fact, much to my surprise, she actually moved her left arm at the end of the surgery. But, currently the injuries that she has sustained have rendered her a quadriplegic. That means that, right now, she is paralyzed from the neck down. Medically speaking, there is no way that she will ever regain any movement below the neck, but, there is a higher power in Heaven, so don't lose hope. She will be in recovery for several hours, and then will be moved back into her room in intensive care."

Joe, Kay, and Kenneth stood hugging each other and crying as the realization of what the surgeon had said settled in their minds. They hated to leave Joe with this weight on his shoulders, but Kay and Kenneth would have to return to Tullahoma. It was Christmas Eve and they had children. They also needed to check on Joey, Jason, and Julie.

After the surgery, Janice was returned to her room. When she awoke from recovery she could tell that she was still paralyzed. She lay on her bed praying, "Lord, please don't let me ever feel anger or bitterness. That's not the way I want to live. Lord, I forgive W.J. for what he's done. Thank you, Lord, that Mama and I survived the shooting. I'll make the best of whatever lies ahead, but please, Lord, let me walk again." Peace entered the room and Janice felt God's hand on her shoulder as she heard His voice say, *"You will walk again, child."*

Joey, Jason and Julie spent Christmas eve with Kay and Kenneth and their two girls, six-year-old Kim and two-year-old Jada. On Christmas morning, they opened all their presents and Santa Claus gifts at Joe and Wilma's house. The usual joy that lives in the hearts of children over Christmas was not apparent. They went through the motions, but their hearts were far from joyful.

After Christmas, Kay and Kenneth got the flu. They insisted that Julie stay with them even though she was exposed to the flu, but they thought that it would be best for the boys to stay with someone that couldn't be found by the Quicks. There were rumors that Mr. and Mrs. Quick would try to take custody of W.J.'s children. Joey and Jason were sent to stay with their former neighbors, Bonnie and Billy. Back in the summer, they had bought another house and moved away from the neighborhood. Joey and Jason had visited their new home several times when their mama was trying to escape W.J. for a day. It was an older house that Bonnie and Billy had renovated into a beautiful country retreat. Joey and Jason loved the quiet, peaceful atmosphere and made themselves right at home. They loved the feeling of being in a whole, healthy family.

The Saturday after the shooting, Janice and Wilma both came out of intensive care. They were assigned a regular room together. At least Joe wouldn't have to split his time between two rooms. He could be with both of them at once.

They were keeping Wilma very sedated due to her internal injuries. Because of this, she didn't recognize the fact that she was in the room with Janice.

"Mama, how are you feeling today?" Janice asked her the second day they were in the room together.

Wilma turned her head away from Janice.

Oh no! She's mad at me! She's not speaking to me because she blames me for getting her shot. Lord, what do I do? Janice thought. It was another whole day before Wilma woke up enough to realize that it was Janice talking to her.

That day a nurse came in with Wilma's lunch and placed it on the bedside table. Most of the time, Wilma slept through mealtime or didn't feel like eating, so it would sit there until it was picked up. Janice, on the other hand, hadn't eaten in eight days. She had an NG tube and couldn't eat, but that didn't keep her from being hungry. *Boy, that lunch smells good,* Janice thought. *I wish now that I had eaten dinner before the Christmas program last week.* Janice had lost a lot of weight, but she hadn't lost her sense of humor.

Since they were in a regular room, Jason and Julie were allowed to visit for the first time, so one week after the shootings, Kenneth and Kay drove the children to Nashville.

Nothing could have prepared Jason for what he saw. He stood transfixed in the doorway, his face turning pale and looking as though he might faint. Nobody looked the same. His Nanny was very weak and frail-looking, and her hair had turned gray almost overnight. His Mama had always been very fair and petite, but after the trauma of being shot and the extensive surgery that she had endured, she was extremely swollen and bruised. Kenneth was holding Julie and she started crying immediately when they entered the room.

"Kenneth, why don't you take Jason and Julie downstairs," Janice said. It was heart-wrenching to see them so traumatized.

The next few days there was a constant string of visitors. Everyone that knew them was so grateful that Janice and Wilma had survived the shooting that they just wanted to show their gratitude and support by making the long drive to Nashville. Janice, Wilma, and Joe were touched by the outpouring of love, however, they were so exhausted that there was no joy in visiting and they quickly tired of answering the usual questions.

The most frustrating part of any long hospital stay is the boredom. Even though they had many visitors, visiting hours were very short and the rest of the time there was nothing to do, especially for a caregiver. You want to help people recover, but it is just a process that has to take its own sweet time. Joe understood the boredom and the long process. It was nearing two weeks since the shooting. He had been there through every minute of it. He watched some television, the traffic outside the window, or his wife and daughter. There was little else to do. One afternoon, Joe was sitting near Janice's bed doing nothing in particular, when he saw her foot move.

"Janice! Your foot is moving!" he shouted as he ran into the hall calling for a nurse. The nurse followed an excited Joe back into the room

"Look! Her foot is moving," he told the nurse as he pointed to the bed.

The nurse pulled the cover back to reveal Janice's foot. It was moving but, upon further examination, it was just a muscle spasm. Even the nurse was disappointed. This emotional rollercoaster was the very reason that Joe lost twenty-five pounds the first two weeks after the shooting. The exuberant expectations of the highs, and the heart rending despair of the lows was enough to steal anyone's appetite.

Joe pulled himself back together after such a let down and began to pack their meager hospital belongings for the trip home the next day. At least they would be back home where he could check on his grandchildren and maybe get a good night's sleep.

"Janice, what's this?" he asked as he held up a small white ziplock bag.

"I don't know. Where did you find it?" she asked.

"It was in this stack of clothes and shoes," Joe answered.

"Well, bring it over here and open it so we can see what it is," Janice said.

Joe opened the small bag and pulled the contents up to the top so that Janice could see.

"My hair?!" Janice exclaimed. Inside the bag was the red hair that she saw fall to the floor in the operating room.

"Who in the world thought I would want to keep that? Throw that stuff in the garbage," she instructed Joe.

On Sunday, two weeks after the shootings, Janice, Wilma, and a weary Joe returned to Tullahoma. The same day, Bonnie and Billy returned Joey and Jason to Kay's house. The Christmas break was over and school would start again on Monday.

Chapter 10

Even though they were still in the hospital, it felt more like home to be back in Tullahoma. Wilma and Janice were in separate rooms and continued to have visitors daily and Joe was able to sleep in his own bed at night. His employer had been very understanding and had willingly let him take off whatever amount of time he needed.

Just a few nights after retuning to Tullahoma, the nurse entered the room to check on Wilma.

"If you don't get her back to Nashville, she's going to die," Wilma's nurse told the charge nurse that night.

They rushed in to check her and called the doctor. She had developed a severe infection and was returned immediately to Nashville for additional surgery and another week's hospital stay. Joe went back to Nashville with his wife.

The first few weeks that Janice was back in Tullahoma were full of turmoil and frustration. Some of the Quick family had been threatening the Hampton family since the shootings. They had it in their heads that Kenneth had shot W.J. Of course this wasn't true, and the police report clearly stated what had happened, but when your tendency is toward violence and you are hurting over the loss of a child, you'll do and say crazy things. At one point, a bomb threat was called in to the hospital, so visiting hours were cut short that day.

After Wilma and Joe returned from Nashville, the Quick family called Janice's attorney to set up an appointment to file for custody of the children. The attorney called Joe and requested he come to the meeting.

"We want to file for custody of W.J.'s children. We don't believe that Janice Quick is a fit mother," Mr. Quick stated to the attorney in front of Joe. He gave no reason for his statement.

"Do you really want to go to court against Joe Hampton?" The attorney asked Mr. Quick.

Mr. and Mrs. Quick thought about that for a few minutes. They knew that Joe was very respected in Tullahoma and going to court against him could prove to be disastrous. So, they offered a solution.

"Well, if Joe will become a legal guardian for the children, then we will be satisfied with that."

Janice agreed for Joe to become a legal guardian, if she didn't lose her rights as their mother. They filed the paperwork and put the process in motion.

During this time the children lived with Kay and Kenneth. They lived in the school district that the boys had been in since 1st grade and it was decided that they should finish out the year in the school in which they were familiar. The school board approved this, agreeing that Joey and Jason were facing enough change in their lives.

They allowed Joey to finish 5th grade and 6th grade at the current school. Jason was permitted to finish the 3rd grade, but in the fall he would transfer to the school that was across the street from Wilma and Joe. It was certain that, until Janice could walk again, they would have to live with either Joe and Wilma or with Kay and Kenneth. Joe and Wilma had a three bedroom house with only two people in it. Kay and Kenneth had their own two children in a smaller house so, Joe and Wilma's was the better option long term. However, since Wilma wasn't able to take care of them yet, they were staying with Kay until the school year was over.

Following her recovery from the second surgery, Wilma remained at Harton hospital in Tullahoma for two more weeks before being dismissed. Although she was nowhere near completely well, Wilma knew when she returned home that she had a lot of preparing to do. To her, there was no question that Janice and the children would live with them. They had to turn two of their three bedrooms into a home. They fixed one bedroom for Joey and Jason, moving their own things from their house into the new room. The other bedroom would be for Janice and Julie. They made sure that Julie had all her familiar things around her to help the four-year-old adjust to this new way of life.

Everyone involved knew, no matter how hard they tried to make the transition easy for the children, it was going to be difficult. When Joey and Jason returned to school, nobody knew how the other children would react to them. It was certain that many of them would have heard about the shootings. Kids have a tendency to speak their minds, ask questions and sometimes be cruel. Joey and Jason needed none of those options. The first day back, their teachers each asked Joey and Jason to work on a special project for them. While they were occupied, the principal met with the school body.

"I'm sure most of you have heard about the tragedy that struck Joey and Jason Quick's family over Christmas. Now, I want each and every one of you to listen closely to me. I don't want anyone talking to them about this or asking them any questions. Don't even mention it to either Joey or Jason. They've had a very hard Christmas break and they don't need to talk about it. Do you understand? Anyone that speaks to them about it will be sent to my office. Dismissed," the principal said.

Thankfully, the children obeyed. Joey picked back up with his school work and, while he was at school, he acted as if nothing had happened. Jason had a little more trouble. He found himself just sitting in class and crying most days. It took a while before he was able to put it behind him during school hours.

The only difference in the way people treated the boys was the number of sleepover invitations they got. Mothers of their friends, and even people that they didn't know, would often call and ask permission for one of the boys to spend the night at their house. Of course, Kay and Kenneth didn't know any of these people. They thought it was best to keep the kids with them and turned down the invitations.

Even though Janice was still hospitalized, the legal

process after W.J.'s death continued. There was an unexpected life insurance policy that Janice knew nothing about and the bank was going to liquidate the store's inventory. Any money above the banknote was to be put in an account for the children.

Janice tried to participate in the legal decisions as much as possible. The vice president of the bank was in charge of processing W.J.'s estate and Janice talked to him often.

"Trader's National Bank, may I help you?" The receptionist answered the phone.

"I'd like to speak to Mr. Copeland, please," Janice said.

"May I ask who's calling?" she asked.

"Janice Quick."

"Hello, Janice," Mr. Copeland answered the phone.

"Hi Phil, I wanted to ask you a question. When you start liquidating the store inventory, could I please give a refrigerator to Mrs. Quick?" Janice asked their longtime banker.

"Janice, I think that would be a very nice thing to do," Phil answered.

"Would you pick one out for me? Give her one that has an automatic ice maker," Janice said.

"I'll do that. I'll pick it out and have it sent to her before we start the liquidation."

"Thank you Phil," Janice said as Wilma hung up the phone for her.

There was a knock on the door.

"Come in," Janice said.

The door opened and in came a young man in a wheelchair.

"Jim!" Janice exclaimed.

"Hi, Janice. Do you feel up to having a visitor?" he asked.

"Of course," Janice answered.

Jim was three years older than Janice. She had admired him in school and was greatly impressed when he was named 'Mr. THS'. After high school, Jim enrolled at the University of Tennessee at Knoxville. He was in his sophomore year and returning to UT after the Christmas break when he hit a slick spot of ice and wrecked his car. The injury left him a quadriplegic. He had been in a wheelchair for ten years. With the help of his mother, he had finished his education and was now working locally as a psychologist.

"How are you feeling, Janice?" Jim asked.

"Good days and bad," she answered. Janice realized that she was having a hard time looking at Jim while they were talking. She didn't want to see him like that, but worse than that, every time she looked at him, she could see herself in that chair. They visited for a while and then Janice couldn't take it any longer.

"How can you accept a wheelchair?" Janice finally asked him with tears in her eyes.

"You have no choice. You just have to live with it," he stated matter-of-factly. In visiting with Jim, Janice saw the potential reality of her situation. It was very disturbing.

While at Harton, Janice developed a problem that was unrelated to her injuries. The first doctor to see her after her return from Baptist Hospital, prescribed four to six shots of Demerol a day. Janice quickly developed a dependence on the drug. Carol, a friend of Kay's, was one of Janice's nurses. She noticed the addiction and posted a sign on her door.

'NOTICE: Do not administer Demerol to this patient'

The day she posted the sign, Carol met Joe at the elevator when he came to visit.

"Mr. Hampton, you might get mad at me, but I've done something to help Janice in the long run," she said.

"What's that, Carol?"

"She has developed an addiction to Demerol. The doctor has prescribed way too much for her small body size. I've stopped all Demerol injections. I'm sorry if that makes you mad, but the last thing Janice needs is a drug addiction."

"I agree, Carol. Thank you for catching this and stopping the drug. We will never know what kind of future problems you may have saved her from," Joe said. When Joe entered Janice's room, she was shaking. Over the next few days, she went through severe withdrawals. At times the entire bed shook as she sweated out the addiction. In near delirium, she would beg for anything to help her, but nothing would help but time. Within a week, the withdrawals subsided and Janice knew that she had beaten the prescription drug addiction.

After six week in the hospital in Tullahoma, there was talk of sending Janice to a special physical rehabilitation facility. Wilma knew that if they did that, Janice wouldn't be home for Easter, so she went shopping.

"Look what I brought for you to see," Wilma said, as she entered Janice's hospital room that day. She had three little dresses for Janice to pick from for Julie's Easter dress.

"I don't think those will fit me," Janice teased her mama, "but I think they would look great on Julie."

Janice picked the one she liked. Wilma knew what it was like to be separated from a grown child, but to have to leave your young children would be even harder. She wanted Janice to still be a part of everyday decisions involving the children as much as possible.

Janice remained in the hospital until March, when she was transferred to a rehab center in Warm Springs, Georgia. In 1974, it was reportedly one of the top locations in the country for physical and occupational therapy and was located two hours south of Atlanta. President Franklin D. Roosevelt originally founded Warm Springs as a rehabilitation facility to treat polio victims. The services offered were later expanded to include amputees, spinal cord and brain injury patients.

Janice felt that she was not ready for rehab, and she certainly wasn't ready to be separated from her family any longer. She was still bleeding through her kidneys and she was still reeling from the shock of what had happened. However, if she had to go, she was determined to make the best of it.

"Where you going, Mama?" a tearful Julie asked her.

"Mama has to go away for a little while to a place

that's going to make me better. When I get back, we will have all sorts of fun," Janice answered.

A six-hour ambulance ride was not really an option for Janice, so Wilma's brother, William, offered to fly her down in his small plane. He, and his business partner owned the plane, but William wasn't able to fly anymore due to a pace-maker. So, Dale, a family friend, flew Janice to Warm Springs, accompanied by Joe and Kay. Wilma wanted to go but was still too weak to make the trip. On March 2, 1975, Jason's ninth birthday, Janice was admitted to the rehab facility.

It was also time for Joe to return to work. Arnold Engineering Development Center had been extremely good to Joe during this tragic time. At this time there was no Family Medical Leave Act to help employees, however, they had allowed him to take two months off, with pay, to care for his family.

Janice's schedule during the months at Warm Springs was very rigorous. She had physical and occupational therapy daily, but she was sick much of the time. She was placed on the bottom floor of the patient room section. It was closer to the physical and occupational therapy areas, but the bottom floor was not the safest place, in Janice's estimation. There were many people around her, but they all seemed to be drug addicts that were there for rehab from accidents or injuries caused by their drug use. At all hours of the day and night, she could hear people in the hall shouting and yelling. There was one incident where a knife was thrown and stuck in the door of a patient's room. Janice did not feel safe at all in her new surroundings. Thankfully, she was so tired at the end of each day that she fell asleep quickly.

Prior to the rehab center she had started moving her head, but after arriving in Georgia, the extremely painful therapy began to pay off when she regained some movement in her arms.

"Well, I know that you've gotten minimal movement back in your arms, but you will never be able to hold a book," the occupational therapist told her one day.

Oh yeah! I'll show you! Janice thought.

That afternoon, Janice sent someone out to buy a book for her to read over the weekend. She labored all weekend to hold the book. It was very difficult to maneuver it and turn the pages, but she managed to read the whole thing.

"I read a book this weekend," Janice told the therapist on Monday morning.

"You did what?" she asked.

"I read a book. I held it and I turned the pages and I read the whole thing," Janice said proudly.

"Well, what an accomplishment! That's great, Janice. With your determination, you will do well in rehabilitation," the therapist encouraged her.

That evening she talked to Wilma on the phone.

"I read a book!" Janice exclaimed. "I held it and I read the whole thing this weekend. I think this is a turning point for me."

"That's wonderful, Janice. You are obviously making progress. How are you feeling physically and emotionally?" Wilma asked her.

"I'm feeling better. It's hard to be away from y'all, but I'm ready to fight this thing. I'm determined, through prayer and hard work, that I will be walking when I get back home."

The days at Warm Springs continued to crawl by. Many days were spent trying to keep Janice's rising temperature down. During these hard times, Francis, a good friend of Wilma's, had a friend from Florida who had been keeping up with Janice's progress. She was traveling through Georgia on her way north and wanted to stop at Warm Springs to meet Janice. She and her husband made their way to her room and were shocked to walk in and find Janice packed in ice.

"Why is she in ice?" she asked the nurse.

"Her temperature is 105 and we've got to lower it as quickly as possible," the nurse answered her.

The couple left immediately and drove the rest of the way to Tennessee. When they arrived, she made a phone call.

"Hi Francis, we stopped to visit Janice on the way through and you need to call her parents. She's going to die down there if they don't do something. They have her packed in ice to bring down a 105 degree fever!"

Francis called Wilma to pass on the news from her friend. They were terrified and called Warm Springs immediately. They were assured that Janice's fever was on the way down and that she would be fine. The high fever caused Janice to miss many days of therapy. However, each time Janice's temperature returned to normal, the physical therapy would continue.

One very gentle therapist was working her legs one day.

"That hurts!" Janice said.

"I'm sorry, Janice, but I didn't do anything different than what I've been doing. I'll be more gentle," she replied.

But every time she moved her left leg a certain way, Janice shouted with pain.

"Doctor, I think I've hurt one of the patients during therapy," the therapist said to Janice's doctor a couple of days later.

"Which one?" he asked.

"Janice Quick. She complains of severe pain when I move her left leg a certain way," she said.

"Well, it's hard to believe that she's experiencing pain, but let me know when your next therapy session is and I will slip in and watch," he told her.

During the next therapy time, the doctor watched and saw just what was happening whenever Janice experienced pain. He realized that somehow Janice's pain was real, so he x-rayed her leg and found out that her hip was broken. The therapist had to change her physical exercise routine to accommodate this break. There was nothing else to be done for it. They couldn't set the bone, so they had to be careful with it until it mended back together.

She also had a problem with her left eye. She had not been able to open it since the shooting. If anyone raised her eyelid up, she could see. She just couldn't open it intentionally. While at Warm Springs, they tried

using an experimental eye drop and her eye started opening and closing like normal. The eye drop brought great
relief to Janice; however, her eye never dilated again. It
wasn't certain if that was caused by the experimental
drops or by the gun shot.

Janice was prescribed many medications while at
Warm Springs. Each week when the medications were
dispensed, she had both a doctor and a pharmacist attending to her. She ended up with 45 pills a day and her
weight dropped to 70 pounds. Since the shooting, Janice
had also not stopped sweating. She sweated twenty-four
hours a day, and had to have her bed changed several
times each day due to this phenomenon. Strangely
enough, continual sweating is an unfortunate symptom of
spinal injury.

Janice cried her way through her time at Warm
Springs rehab center. The therapy was excruciating. She
was regaining feeling in her arms and legs and movement
in her arms, but her legs were still not cooperating. Many
of the days she would pray, 'God, please help me get
through today', and at the end of the day she would realize, 'I did make it through the day'. Although she had
heard all along what the many doctors had said, Janice
truly felt that she would walk. However, as the months
dragged by and there was no muscle control developing
in her legs, Janice was beginning to lose hope of walking
again.

The time had come to go home.

"Hello, is this Mrs. Joe Hampton?" The doctor
asked Wilma.

"Yes, this is she," Wilma replied.

"I'm one of Janice's doctors from Warm Springs Rehab Center. I was calling to inform you that she is ready to come home," he said.

"That's great! She's walking!" Wilma shouted in joy.

"No ma'am. She's not walking. She will never walk again," the doctor reluctantly told her.

"Oh, I see," Wilma said as her voice broke. "We will make arrangements to come get her in the next couple of days," she said as she hung up. Wilma felt as if the wind had been knocked out of her. She cried for hours at the thought that all hope for Janice to walk again was lost. She knew that the Lord could supernaturally do what he wanted to with her, but it wasn't looking good in the natural.

Joe and Wilma tried to arrange another flight for Janice, but Dale was working full time and there was no one else available to fly. So, Joe and Wilma drove down to Warm Springs to bring her home.

On June 10, 1975, Janice retuned to Tullahoma in a wheelchair.

Joey, Jason, and Julie
March 1975

Chapter 11

Home Again

Returning home after such intensive physical rehabilitation was a culture shock. Janice had grown used to doctors, nurses, and pharmacists as her daily companions. She had developed a great deal of confidence and reliance upon these individuals. However, when she returned home, her parents were in charge of her physical well being. They had to do everything for her and she had to learn to trust them for her care as she had come to trust the healthcare professionals. It was a difficult time of adjustment.

Reality was also sinking in. Janice awoke every day with the expectation that she would walk that day, but the days were turning into months with no sign of the miracle that she needed. Her frustration grew to the point of despair.

God, why did you tell me I would walk again? I know I heard your voice. I know that you said I would walk again, but every day there's no improvement. Why do you get my hopes up only to dash them every morning? Janice poured her frustrations out to the Lord in heart wrenching sobs. When the crying finally quieted down, she heard a still small voice say, *I didn't tell you that it would be on earth.* Realization dawned on her and the peace that only Jesus can give flooded her troubled soul. She understood. He hadn't left her or purposefully tormented her. He had spoken peace and encouragement to her in her darkest hour. She knew that she could live this life without ever walking again, as long as the Lord was with her.

Janice found that her relationship with the Lord was growing daily, and her prayer life was increasing. She had always prayed for her children, but since the shootings, she prayed fervently for them. Her most urgent prayer was for peace over the harsh circumstances of their lives.

Lord, please deliver my children from the effects of W.J.'s abuse. They are still young and you, Lord, can break this destructive cycle. Jesus, forgive me for not getting them out sooner. I pray, Lord, that there's still time for them to have a good childhood. Lord, please don't let them grow up to be abusive like their father. Give them peace and protect them. Cause them to be good parents and good spouses. Father, bring them to the place that you have for them and grow them into the plans that you have for their lives.

Joey and Jason had endured a hard year since the shootings. They were having to adjust to a new location, a new way of life, and, in Jason's case, a new school starting in the fall. Wilma had been talking on the phone to Janie, one of Joe's relatives in East Tennessee, and Janie had offered to have them come visit for the summer.

"Janice, I was just talking to Janie and she has invited Joey and Jason to spend the summer with them. What do you think about that?" Wilma asked.

"Wow. I think that would be great. I would miss not seeing them this summer, but it would be a lot of fun for them. Call them in here and let's ask them," she suggested. The boys had been playing outside and came running in the door.

"How would the two of you like to spend the rest of the summer in East Tennessee with Janie?" Janice asked them.

"You mean we could go for a whole month?" Jason asked.

"Yes."

"That would be so cool. Do you think she would take us to Gatlinburg?" Joey asked.

"Probably."

"I'm in."

"Me too!" Jason said.

"Mama, could you please call Janie and work out the details? We need to get these guys up there so they don't miss another day of vacation."

"Can I go too, Mama?" Julie asked.

"No, sweetheart, you have to stay here. What would I do without my big helper? You know how much it helps me to have you get water for me, and wash my face, and fix my hair," Janice said.

"Joey, I can't go because I have to help Mama," four-year-old Julie explained to her big brother as she walked out of the room.

Before the boys left for their vacation, there was another hurdle for Janice to cross. She hadn't been to church since the shootings. She was strong enough now to sit in a wheelchair for a couple of hours so the family decided it was time to return to Sunday services. Janice was nervous. Several of the church members blamed her for the divorce. Of course, most of them knew nothing of the horror that she had faced for the past twelve years. Still she wasn't sure she would be welcomed or accepted back into their fellowship.

"Mama, I'm nervous about going to church. Isn't that crazy? Why would anybody be scared to go to their own church?" Janice asked as Wilma dressed her that morning.

"Don't be nervous. You know that the people at church love you. Look how much they've done for us since all this happened! There's not a day goes by that somebody from church doesn't check on us or drop by. They love you and are very excited for us all to be back in services," Wilma assured her.

Janice knew that everything Wilma said was true, but it still didn't keep her from being apprehensive. They arrived before services started and several people came by to speak to her or pat her on the back and tell her it was great to see her again, but she was still experiencing an underlying tension. The song leader started the service with a familiar hymn. Before he started the second song, he looked straight at Janice.

"Janice, we are singing this one just for you," he

said as he called out the hymnal page number. It was a beautiful old song that was perfect for her situation and all she had endured. A song celebrating the goodness of God and his ever-present loving care. Tears flooded Janice's eyes as the entire congregation turned toward her and sang. Her fears were unfounded, they all welcomed her back.

After Joey and Jason left for East Tennessee, Wilma and Joe took Janice to the doctor in Nashville for a routine check up. Janice had so many different specialists that trips to Nashville were becoming very frequent. Joe's sister lived near Nashville and they wanted to stop by her house to visit after the doctor's appointment. Joe's dad lived with her. He was suffering from Parkinson's disease and because of the disease, he had started showing signs of dementia. For the previous several years before the shootings, he had been alternating months staying with Joe and Joe's sister. Afterward, he had stayed solely with Joe's sister due to the stress that Joe and Wilma were under. Wilma was still recovering, and learning to provide for Janice's needs and the children kept her plate full.

"Come on in," Sis said, as she opened the door.

Joe pushed Janice in her wheelchair into the living room where Papa Hampton was sitting. Janice was particularly excited about coming to her aunt's house because she hadn't seen her Grandpa since the shootings.

"Hi, Papa!" Janice said grinning from ear to ear.

He looked up with a shocked expression on his face and then his eyes filled with tears. When he finally spoke, his voice cracked.

"I thought you were dead and they just didn't tell me," he cried.

Janice was heartbroken at the thought that he had believed for eight months that his oldest grandchild was dead.

"No, Papa. I'm paralyzed, but I'm still alive," Janice explained to him.

After seeing how much it meant to Papa Hampton to see Janice, Joe and his sister decided to try letting him coming back to Tullahoma every other month.

It had been over a month since she returned from Warm Springs, and Janice had been managing very well. She maintained her schedule of exercise and kept active to try to increase her mobility. However, the activity didn't keep her from being ill. She developed a severe kidney infection and was sent to Vanderbilt Hospital in Nashville. During the week that she was there, she had a surprise visitor. Her neurosurgeon from Baptist Hospital found out that she was at Vanderbilt and dropped by to see her.

"Hey!" Janice said, waving her arms in the air as he entered her room. She continued to wave them at him.

"I see you! I see what you're doing," he said with a huge smile. "It's great to see that you have movement back. I would like you to meet Dr. Brooks," he said motioning to the man that had entered the room with him.

"Hello, Dr. Brooks," Janice said.

"Hi, Janice, I've heard a great deal about you," he replied.

"Janice, Dr. Brooks pioneered the surgery for treating people with severely injured hands, such as yourself, and I wanted him to meet you," the neurosurgeon explained. "But, I would also like to test your nerve responses," he said, smiling again as he pulled the dreaded safety pin out of his pocket.

"Oh, not the pin. I have feeling back everywhere," Janice grimaced.

"Can you feel this?" He said as he poked the pin into her leg.

"YES!" She shouted.

"How about here?" He asked poking her abdomen.

"YES again!" She said. "Would you please stop poking me with that infernal pin! I told you I have feeling back everywhere and that thing hurts!"

The doctors both laughed at her, enjoying the fact that she had regained feeling over her entire body.

"We will be talking some more about your hand surgeries after you've had a little more time to recuperate," her doctor told her as he and Dr. Brooks left the room.

Once her kidney infection was under control, Janice was sent home. Things at home were settling into a daily routine. Wilma and Joe had proved to be excellent caregivers. They didn't have the medical background of the people Janice had come to rely on at Warm Springs, but they had something that no one else had, a love for Janice that exceeded human understanding. They were displaying perfect parental love, sacrificing their own individual lives for their child. Wilma and Joe were well aware of the possible commitment of having to take care of

Janice for the rest of their lives, but in their minds, there was no other option. They had brought her into the world and they would do whatever was necessary to make sure that she was properly cared for.

Joey and Jason came back from their East Tennessee vacation about the time that Janice came back home from Vanderbilt Hospital.

"We had the best time! Janie and her husband Gerry took us to the University of Tennessee!! We got to go out on the field and into the locker room and everything! We even got to meet some of the players," Joey excitedly told Janice.

"Yeah, and we even got to meet the Coach! Did you know that Janie is his secretary? That was amazing! I can't wait to tell the guys at school that my cousin is Coach Major's secretary," Jason added.

They couldn't talk fast enough to tell her all the cool things that they did. It was obviously just what they needed.

"And Janie said she wanted us to come back next summer. She said we were very well behaved and that we kept our room clean," Joey said.

"What? Kept your room clean? Why can't you do that here?" Wilma teased them.

"Mama, can we go back next summer too?" Jason pleaded.

"Well......"

"Please, please, please!" They begged.

"Of course you can go back next summer," Janice couldn't stand to see them agonizing over the decision since she had already decided they could go.

"YES!" They shouted as they high fived each other and then ran out of the room to play.

"Remind me to give Janie a call and let her know how much the summer meant to Joey and Jason," Janice said to Wilma. "I'm happy they got to go, but I'm even happier that they're back."

Janice had been home from Vanderbilt for a month, when Wilma noticed something unusual.

"Janice, look at your legs, they are bent as if you were sitting in a chair," Wilma said.

Janice looked at her legs. They were bent.

"Did you pull your legs up?" Wilma asked with hope rising in her voice.

"I don't think so," Janice answered.

"Well, try to move them and see what happens."

Janice tried and tried but could not get her legs to move. "I can't move them, so they must have done that on their own."

Wilma gently tried to move her legs back down into a straight position.

"I can't move them either," Wilma said with all hope gone from her voice but a hint of anxiety creeping in.

"Don't push too hard, Mama, you might break something. Why don't we wait until Daddy gets home from work and see what he thinks," Janice suggested.

When Joe got home, he went straight to Janice's bedside.

"What seems to be the problem with these unruly

legs," he said, trying to lighten the mood.

"I don't know. Mama noticed that they were bent like that, but I didn't do it," Janice explained.

Joe tried to push her legs back down also, but they were so set that he couldn't force them down onto the bed.

"Joe, I think they are more bent than they were this morning. Maybe we should call the doctor," Wilma suggested.

They contacted the doctor and he ordered her to be sent back to Vanderbilt. Her muscles were drawing up and shrinking from lack of use, which caused her legs to draw up towards her chest. Two surgeries were necessary to alleviate the problem She was cut from her groin to her hip bone on both legs and then placed in casts up to her thighs.

She was awakened during surgery by the staff shouting at her.

"Why didn't you tell us you were a free bleeder? You are bleeding badly!"

Janice came around long enough to say, "I didn't know".

The surgical team managed to get the bleeding under control to finish the surgery. They placed a spreader bar between her ankles to keep her legs straight and apart. The doctor accompanied her back to her room to insure that her legs were placed properly. They had to turn her on her side to get her feet through the doorway. Once in the room, her legs were so far apart at the feet that they had to place folding chairs on either side of her bed on which to rest her feet.

The doctor ordered a trapeze bar to be mounted hanging over the bottom half of her bed. Every two hours she was turned on her side with one foot placed in the bar. Janice remained in the hospital for two months. During this time a young counselor named Jane started visiting her. Janice had built a huge wall around her heart and she didn't want anyone trying to dismantle it. It simply hurt too much to deal with the pain. But Jane was determined to get in. While at Warm Springs, Janice had developed the habit of sleeping with the sheet pulled up over her head. She started this out of necessity. The eye drops that she was prescribed caused the light to make her eyes burn, so covering her face became a way to relieve the burning. After a while, it became her way of sleeping. Whenever Janice knew that it was time for Jane to stop by her room, she would pull the sheet up over her head as if she were asleep. It didn't take Jane long to see through this.

"Janice, I know you are not asleep," Jane said as she pulled a chair up to Janice's bedside. "I'm not married so I've got no one waiting on me. I'll stay here all night if I have to."

Janice finally gave in and pulled the sheet down. "Okay, we can talk."

And for weeks and weeks they talked. Finally, Jane broke through the wall of Janice's heart and she began the long journey of emotional healing. Jane brought her out of a fantasy world and set her feet in reality. While at Vanderbilt, she was also taken off the forty-five pills a day that she had been taking. This time when she returned home, Janice felt like her old self. Being off the drugs, and having her heart opened was a life changer for her.

Janice returned home in mid-October 1975. The children were adjusting to their new home at Nanny and Daddy Joe's house, but Janice was struggling. As much as she wanted to be out going places, she found herself more and more reluctant to leave the house and go out in public. She felt 'dirty' from all of the abuse and violence that she had suffered. Janice also knew that she was now different than most of the people that she passed in public. The muscular control in her hands and arms wasn't fully functional yet and because of that, she got a lot of curious stares. The extra attention of being in public was just too much added stress. But time, the Lord, and a determined family, got her over some very big hurdles.

Joe had purchased a van that would accommodate Janice's wheelchair, so they took a trip to East Tennessee to visit relatives. When they stopped in Chattanooga for breakfast, Janice started getting nervous. She was embarrassed to eat in public because she usually made a very bad mess when she tried to feed herself. Her arms and hands had movement, but the fine motor skills were still lacking.

"Okay everybody, this looks like a good restaurant, let's eat breakfast," Joe said as he got out of the van and headed around to Janice's side door. "Are you ready to eat?" He asked her as he opened the door.

"No, I'm not really hungry. I'll just stay in the van. Y'all go ahead and have a good breakfast," Janice said.

She was so hungry her stomach was growling, but some things are worse than hunger pains.

"What do you mean you're not hungry? You haven't eaten yet," Joe said a little confused.

"I'm just not hungry. Go ahead and don't worry about me," Janice answered him.

Joe walked over and talked to Kay and Kenneth for a few minutes and then came back to the van with Kenneth.

"Sorry, Janice, you're going in and you're going to eat. You've got to face being in public sooner or later. This looks like a good place to start," Joe said as he and Kenneth removed her from the van.

She waited anxiously after placing her order for the food to come. *Didn't they understand how embarrassing it was to not be able to feed yourself?* she thought as the waitress set her plate in front of her. Wilma strapped the fork apparatus to her right hand and the moment of truth was here. Janice slowly and deliberately scooped the food onto the fork and brought it to her mouth. She didn't drop it. *Don't get excited, that was only one bite,* she told herself, but the rest of the meal went well. Janice was extremely proud because, for the first time, she hadn't made a mess. This seemed to be one of the last stumbling blocks that she faced. She was now ready to accept whatever was placed in front of her.

During November, Joe and Wilma added a large room onto their house for Julie and Janice. The proceeds from the sale of Janice's house paid for the addition, so Joe and Wilma added to their will that Janice was to be reimbursed the cost of the addition, whenever their house was sold after their deaths. The men of the church constructed the addition for the family. The room was big enough for Janice's hospital bed, a bed for Julie, an area for Janice's visitors to sit, an entertainment center, a large closet, and a private bathroom. The addition had its own entrance with a wheelchair ramp to make it convenient for Janice to come and go. One-by-one, the obstacles and hurdles that were set before them in the past year were being overcome.

After the first of the year, Janice had some very special visitors. Jane, her counselor from Vanderbilt, and two nurses, drove all the way to Tullahoma to visit her. They were happy to see Janice doing so well.

"Janice, do you have a cold?" one of the nurses asked her.

"Yes, it's so aggravating," Janice answered her.

"You should call your doctor and see if he will prescribe an antihistamine for you," the nurse suggested.

"That's probably a good idea. I certainly don't need a cold on top of everything else," Janice said.

That afternoon Dr. Harvey gave her a prescription for an antihistamine. Her cold began to heal and within two or three days, Janice noticed something else going on in her body. She wasn't sweating anymore! Evidently, the antihistamine had stopped her continuous sweating problem. A few weeks later, Janice was at Vanderbilt for a routine visit and ran into her urologist. She told him what happened with the cold medicine and he said that he might try it with a few of his patients. Later, she found out he had tried the antihistamine treatment on five of his patients that suffered from continuous sweating. Of the five people, two of them were healed like Janice.

In the early spring of 1976, Janice returned to Vanderbilt for surgery on her hands. One hand was curled in toward her wrist and the other was stretched backwards toward her forearm. Dr. Brooks, the doctor that she met the summer before, performed two different surgeries on one of her hands. She returned home to give the hand time to completely heal. After about six months, when it was apparent that her hand had become more usable, they scheduled the same two surgeries on the other hand. They too were successful. Janice had recovered enough use of her hands to make life a little easier.

During the first two years after the shooting, Janice underwent nine major surgeries. She got more proficient with her arm and hand movements but her legs were still unresponsive. The feeling was there, but there was no muscle control.

Wilma, Joe, Janice, Joey, Jason, and Julie had learned to live as a family unit. The children realized that Janice was still their mother, but they came to rely more and more on Wilma and Joe. There were rules that they had to obey, but it was different from their home when W.J. was alive. The rules that Nanny and Daddy Joe made were governed by love and not by anger. When they broke the rules, they were disciplined in a normal, healthy manner. Joey, Jason, and Julie were never yelled at or struck in an inappropriate way ever again. Needless to say, at this point, the children's lives were better than they had ever been.

Joey and Jason were both playing little league. They were on the same team the first year they played, and Kenneth was one of their coaches. They both loved sports but, because of their past abuse, they struggled with performing. Because of this, Joey only played one year, but Jason continued playing for several more years. All three children were active in school, church, and sports. Janice had become so much more mobile now and was able to attend many of their events. Whenever she wasn't able to be there, another family member would attend in her place.

There was a couple in their church that took a real interest in spending time with the boys. Randy was a young preacher, and he and his wife, Earla, didn't have any children of their own. Joey and Jason would frequently stay with them on the weekends. They learned to work on vehicles by helping Randy work on his truck. They helped out around the house and just enjoyed being in a family setting. Daddy Joe was a wonderful role model and 'father' figure, but so much of his time was spent tending to Janice's needs. Being with Randy and Earla felt like a 'normal' home to them, and Joey and Jason had their undivided attention, which was something they needed very much.

Chapter 12

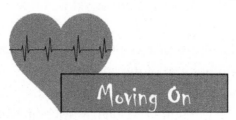

In September 1977, Joey turned fourteen years old and started to work at the local hospital. He performed many different jobs there, including painting, washing dishes in the hospital cafeteria, helping in the dietary department, and delivering trays to patients. He enjoyed working and was very conscientious about his job. Joey was great at saving his money. He knew that it wouldn't be long before he was old enough to have a car and he wanted to have plenty to spend when the time came.

After Julie entered school that same fall, Janice got interested in the possibility of finding a job. Since she had served as a non-paid secretary and bookkeeper for W.J.'s appliance business, she was ineligible for Social Security Disability Insurance. However, she wanted more independence and the capability of earning a living. Janice's children were her life, but she cringed at the thought that they would have to take care of her for the rest of their lives.

Three years earlier, just a month after the shooting, Janice had someone from the Tennessee Department of Human Services contact her about vocational rehabilitation. They had taken an application for possible services. Over the years, she had been in occasional contact with a rehabilitation counselor and it was now time to give her a call.

"Christine Hopkins, please," Janice said to the voice on the other end of the line.

"Hold, please," the voice answered.

"This is Christine Hopkins. May I help you?"

"Yes. This is Janice Quick and you visited me about rehabilitation a couple of times in the last several years. I would like to discuss job opportunities with you. Could you please stop by my house one day?"

"Of course," Christine replied. "Let me check my schedule and we can set a day and time for me to come by. Why are you interested in job opportunities at this time?"

"My youngest just entered school and I want to be productive. The thought of lying in this bed for the rest of my life with nothing to do is very depressing."

"I understand," Christine said. "I can come by next Tuesday at 2 p.m."

"That will be fine," Janice agreed.

The next week Christine arrived and immediately started assessing Janice's interests and capabilities.

"What kind of work would you be interested in?" she asked Janice.

"My first thought was secretarial work. I did that and kept the books for my husband's business for several years. But the more I think about it, the more I realize that I just don't have the hand coordination or muscle control for a job that needs such fine motor skills, so I guess that's out," Janice answered her.

"Well, do you have any other interests that I might explore for you?" Christine asked her.

"Not at this time. I was hoping you would have some ideas," Janice said.

They talked that day and several more times without coming to any possible solution.

For the past two years, Joe's dad had been staying with them every other month. His Parkinson's and dementia had progressed to the place that it was impossible for Wilma to handle. He went back to Joe's sister's house full-time and eventually ended up in a nursing facility. In the early summer of 1978, Joe took the family to visit his dad. They had been there for a few hours when the family decided to get something to eat.

"Janice, are you coming with us to the cafeteria?" Joe asked her.

"No Daddy, y'all go ahead. I'll just sit here and visit with Papa Hampton."

They left the room and Papa Hampton looked at Janice.

"Are you sitting in that wheelchair just for show?" he asked her.

"No, Papa, I have to sit in this wheelchair. Remember my ex-husband shot me and mama and now I can't walk," Janice patiently explained to him.

"Oh yeah! I remember that S.O.B.," he replied. There were moments when he was completely lucid and acting like his old self and then there was the majority of the time when he was in his own world of confusion.

When they returned home from visiting Papa Hampton, Janice registered to take a Communications course at Motlow State Community College in Tullahoma. She had been thinking about the idea for a while and decided that she needed to do something that she could enjoy. She loved the course so much that she considered that some job in communications might be her answer. She discussed it with Christine, but nothing ever presented itself as a viable job possibility. In March of 1979, Christine called Janice about an entirely different matter.

"Hi Janice, how are you doing today?" Christine asked.

"I'm doing fine. How are you?" Janice answered.

"Fine. Janice, I've been thinking about you and there's something that I would like to suggest. I'm involved in the Coffee County Committee for the disabled and we are looking for a disabled lady to sponsor for the Miss Tennessee Wheelchair competition later this spring. I've suggested you," Christine said.

"Me? Are you kidding?" Janice answered, shocked at the idea.

"Yes, you! The lady that won a couple of years ago was from Coffee County and I think you have an excellent chance of winning," she answered.

"Well, if you think that it would be good for me, I'll give it a try."

Janice entered the competition that was scheduled for May and placed 3rd. She was very excited about the accomplishment. Wilma wasn't as happy.

"I was so afraid that you might win and that would mean a lot of traveling for you," Wilma told her after the contest was over.

"Were you pulling for me NOT to win?" Janice asked her.

"Well....kind of," Wilma admitted.

"That's okay, Mama, I'm satisfied with third place," Janice assured her.

Later that summer, Janice was listening to the radio as she did everyday, when she realized that she might enjoy broadcasting. She loved music and the fun that the radio personalities always seemed to have, so she called Christine.

"Christine, I think I've found something that I'm very interested in within the communications field. Radio broadcasting," Janice excitedly told Christine.

"That's great, Janice, I'll look into possible job opportunities in the area and see what the requirements are for a career in broadcasting," Christine said.

She started checking with local radio stations for possible on the job training and discovered that first you have to have a third-class license in broadcast, endorsed by the Federal Communications Commission. A local station promised to hire Janice if she obtained her license.

In preparation for entering school and then the job market, Christine got Janice admitted to the Patricia Neal Rehabilitation Center in Knoxville for further occupational and physical therapy. The Center opened in 1978 and is East Tennessee's recognized leader in rehabilitation for stroke, spinal cord, and brain injury patients. Janice was transported to the facility on October 31, 1979 and stayed until mid-December. She was expecting rehab, but what she got was an intensive exercise program to strengthen her upper body. This was far removed from the three months rehab she had at Warm Springs. The skills she needed to hold a spoon or a book were totally different from the muscles and stamina that she would need to re-enter the job market. Janice discovered muscles that she had forgotten were even there. But, like every other obstacle that she faced, she persevered and finished the six weeks, returning home with new abilities and strength.

Christine also found a nurse to live with Janice while she attended the Tennessee Institute of Broadcasting in Nashville. Janice and her companion/RN, Martha, moved into an apartment near the school. Classes started in March of 1980. Martha, whose job it was to take care of Janice personally, also attended classes with her to help with whatever was needed. Every Friday afternoon, Joe, or sixteen-year-old Joey, would drive to Nashville in Janice's handicap accessible van and pick her up for the weekend. On Sunday afternoon, they would drive her back to the Nashville apartment. During this time she kept in contact with Christine.

"Janice, the Coffee County Committee wants to sponsor you again this year for Miss Tennessee Wheelchair," Christine told her one day in April.

"Christine! You know that I'm in school right now. That would be too much to try to compete again. Anyway, I'm not interested in it."

"Oh, Janice, you might win this year. Please compete one more time," Christine all but begged her.

"My mama told me last year that she didn't want me to win because it would be too much traveling. She'll have a fit if I enter again this year."

"Please, for me...."Christine said.

"Oh, alright! I'll enter again," Janice finally gave in.

It wasn't as much trouble as Janice had originally thought. She was living in Nashville anyway, so it was no big deal to spend a couple of days preparing for the competition.

In May 1980, Janice entered the Miss Tennessee Wheelchair pageant for the second time...and won first place. There was only one problem: Wilma. Now that she had won Miss Tennessee, Janice would have to represent the state in the national competition in late June, in Ohio.

"I told you not to win this thing," Wilma jokingly complained.

"Sorry, Mama, I did everything but frown to keep from winning," Janice teased, "looks like I'll be going to Ohio next month."

"How will the school feel about you missing a week of school the month before your license exam?" Wilma asked her.

"They are so excited about this that they will do whatever is necessary to help me catch up. I'll be ready for the exam when the time comes."

In June, Janice and Martha made the trip to Ohio for the competition. It was Wednesday when they flew out of the Nashville airport and landed in Atlanta. There they

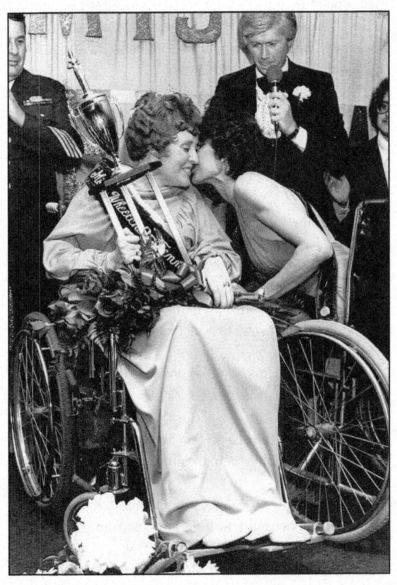

Janice being crowned by the previous
Miss Tennessee Wheelchair

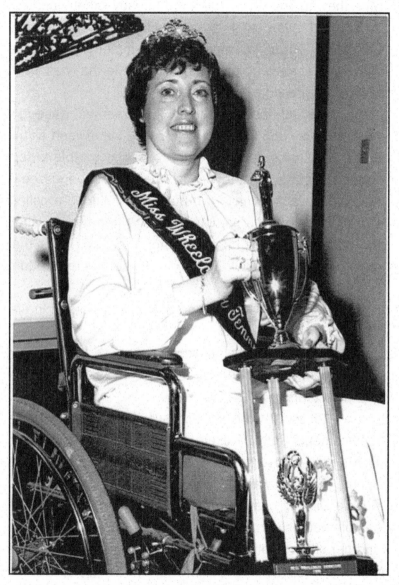

Miss Tennessee Wheelchair 1980

had to change plans to fly on to Columbus, Ohio. By the time they arrived, they were both already exhausted. And so began the hardest thing that Janice could ever remember doing. Thursday morning they immediately started with interviews and photo sessions. Martha was even feeling the pressure.

"This schedule is brutal!" She remarked, while running from one appointment to the next. In between all the media requirements, Janice had to display a table to represent her state. Since everyone knows that Tennessee is famous for Jack Daniel's whiskey, she included a collection of Jack Daniel's sample bottles. When they finished the table, they were off to another interview. Later that day, they stopped back by the Tennessee table to add a few more items.

"The Jack Daniel's is gone!" Janice shouted in disbelief.

"What?!" Martha asked.

"Look! Someone stole most of my display!" Janice was near tears.

"Let's call Christine and see if she can get some replacements sent by express mail," Martha suggested. They called Christine and she told them that she would handle it. She was unable to get Jack Daniel's, but George Dickel, located in Tullahoma, offered to send the sample bottles. Christine brought them with her when she and her children drove to Columbus on Friday. The stress of the interviews, photo sessions, and the great whiskey heist, had Janice exhausted again. She couldn't wait to get to the room that night to get some much needed rest.

Janice knew that Friday morning was going to be very stressful.

The day began with an interview in front of ten judges, including one from Tennessee. Since the contest was based on how each person handled their disability, how they were moving forward, and what they were trying to achieve, Janice was shocked and taken off guard at some of the judges' questions.

"Mrs. Quick," asked one of the judges, "if you had a male friend that you had become close to, including having him around your children, and he announced to you that he was a homosexual, how would you handle that?"

Janice was stunned. *What does this have to do with Miss USA Wheelchair?* She thought. But there was no time to think or form an argument for your opinions.

"Well, due to my Christian values, and to protect my children, I suppose I would have to terminate the friendship," Janice answered them as honestly as she knew how. In Tullahoma, in 1980, the homosexual community was very sparse. As a matter of fact, very few people knew anyone who even knew anyone that was homosexual. It was something that you just didn't think about, because you never had to deal with it.

After the interview, Janice went back to the room to meet her family. Wilma, Joe, Joey, Jason, Julie, Kay, Kenneth, Kim and Jada had arrived to support Janice.

"I think I just lost the pageant, "Janice said as she entered the room. She told them about the interview and the questions. She was disappointed that a social issue, that had nothing to do with her disability or her future plans, could possibly decide her fate in the competition.

Friday evening was the first night of the public part of the pageant. Janice was dressed in the evening gown that she wore for the Miss Tennessee Wheelchair competition and she was escorted by a member of the Naval Reserve. The family was following her as the Reservist wheeled her towards the escalator.

"Ah....I don't think I can go up an escalator," Janice said as she looked up at the Navy officer.

"Don't be surprised," he said, as he grinned at her.

When Wilma realized what he was about to do, she panicked. But before she could stop him, he had positioned Janice's back two wheels on the escalator and tilted her back. She was practically looking straight up at him.

"Wheeeee," she laughed, as the escalator carried her higher and higher. "This is great! I haven't had this much fun in a long time."

Since there were only thirty states represented in the competition, it didn't take long for Janice to be called forward to address the audience and judges. She had 30 seconds to say anything that she wanted to about herself.

"Hello, I'm Janice and I am in school to become a radio disc jockey. One day I hope to be a radio station program director. I am a Christian and I believe that every morning God gives us a brand new day and we can choose to use it for good or choose to let the day go by. I choose to use every day I have for good."

She returned to her spot on the stage to the sound

of applause. Friday night was nearing an end and the next morning would determine who was called back for the top ten.

Saturday morning all the contestants met for a late breakfast before having a tour of the capitol. During the breakfast, the top ten contestants would be announced. Janice held her breath as the names were called out. When she heard her name, she was both shocked and relieved. She had made it into the top ten!

Later that day, she donned the beautiful gown that the state had bought for her as she prepared for the evening competition. While she was waiting outside the stage, the Tennessee judge approached her and began talking. Janice was disturbed by this. As a judge, he wasn't supposed to be talking to any of the contestants. And if that wasn't disturbing enough, he asked her if they could see each other when they returned to Nashville.

"I really don't know. Let's just wait until we get back. I'm really not sure," she said, worried that any interaction, even talking, with a judge would ruin her chances of winning.

The top ten contestants were presented to the audience and judges. They weren't required to do anything during this presentation. Afterwards, they left the stage waiting for the announcement of the top five. There would be a Miss USA Wheelchair, 1st, 2nd, 3rd and 4th place winners.

As Janice left the stage, she passed the trophy and crown sitting on a table. She hadn't given any thought to winning or even wanting to win until then. *I hope I win!*

She thought as she entered the hallway to await the judges decision.

The judges made their decision and Janice was not called back to the stage. Her family made sure that she knew how proud they were of her. It was a great accomplishment to be Miss Tennessee Wheelchair and an honor to compete in the Miss USA Wheelchair pageant. After the presentation of crowns, everyone made their way out of the auditorium. As Janice started down the hall, she heard someone calling her name.

"Janice! Janice!"

She turned around to see the judges approaching her.

"Janice, we would all like to personally invite you back next year for the competition," one of the judges said.

"Well, that's very kind of you. I will certainly think about it," she answered, stunned at this unusual invitation.

Martha took Janice back to their room and helped her get ready for bed.

"You know, when you didn't get called back in the top five, that was the most relaxed I've seen you since the pageant began," she told Janice.

"Yeah, I think it's time to leave this stress behind and get back to Nashville for my license exam," Janice laughed. The next day they started the return trip, from Columbus to Atlanta, then changed planes and flew back to Nashville.

Returning to school, Janice had a few weeks to

prepare for the test. She passed with flying colors and received her broadcasting license. The rest of the summer was spent in interviews and television appearances as Miss Tennessee Wheelchair.

In October 1980, Janice was hired by WBGY-FM in Tullahoma. She was so well-liked that, by Christmas, she was also assigned work shifts on the AM station. She worked from 9 a.m. until noon on the FM station and then from 2-5 p.m. on the AM station Monday through Friday with a six-hour shift on FM on Sundays.

Joey, Jason, and Julie were growing up all too fast. Many times Joey, who was now a senior in high school, drove Janice to work and would stay and help her with her duties. Jason was in his freshman year and he also spent time at the radio station helping Janice, when he wasn't working. At the age of fourteen he had started to work at the local hospital doing the same job that Joey had done. In true teenage boy fashion, Jason saved everything he could for a car. Julie was nine years old and enjoying all the things that hold the interest of a young girl. She loved her dolls, coloring, and taking care of her mother. However, Julie's life was not the life of a typical nine-year-old. She shared a room with her invalid mother and had no opportunity to enjoy a place of her own. She had a front row seat to all of the medical care, treatments and procedures that were performed on Janice daily. Back in the spring, when Janice was preparing to move to Nashville, Julie became ill. After hospitalizing her, the doctor determined it was a nervous stomach. She couldn't stand the thought of being separated from Janice. Julie was always

TRAINING FOR 'DJ' — Jancie Quick, a quadriplegic, wants to work as a disc jockey on radio. She is attending the Tennessee Institute of Broadcasting in Nashville.
— Photos by Margo Turner

The Tullahoma News
March 7, 1980

SHE'S ON THE AIR — Janice Quick of Tullahoma, partially paralyzed for six years, has achieved her goal of becoming a disc jockey. She is now employed full-time at Radio Station WBGY. (Story on Page 2-A.)
— Photo by Margo Turner

The Tullahoma News
January 16, 1981

worried that something bad would happen to Janice if they were apart. Perhaps this was from being separated from her mama for so long after the shootings, or possibly it was from the actual shootings and the many close calls Janice had experienced since. After Janice moved back home and started to work, Julie would often fake an illness to stay out of school. She was afraid that if she went to school, Janice would leave again for some reason. The chaotic and unusual nature of her life was forming some very real struggles within Julie which stayed hidden for years before they were understood.

The big decision looming in front of Joey was what path to take after high school. He thought that some sort of business degree would be good and he was in the process of deciding where the best place was to obtain that degree. Should he go to the local junior college for two years, or move away to a four year university immediately after graduation? He was leaning toward moving away. He longed to make a fresh start where no one knew him or pitied him. He didn't want to be known for the rest of his life as the kid whose dad shot his mom and he figured the best way to accomplish that would be to move directly to a four-year university.

Joey had been dating a young lady named Susan for over a year. Her influence on his life was like a steady hand on his back. She listened to him and tried to offer comfort and direction. She was a year older than Joey and had already graduated from high school and was attending Middle Tennessee State University. This was the closest four-year university to Tullahoma and only an hour away. However, because of the summers he spent in East Tennessee, Joey was a big UT fan. But, the University of Tennessee was four hours away from home and three hours away from Susan. In the end, love won out, and Joey decided to attend MTSU.

As her children's lives grew busier, Janice found great fulfillment in her job. The joy that working brought to Janice was hard to understand for some people. She looked at work in a fresh new way. Those who work daily in the same job for years sometimes forget what a blessing it is to be able to get up in the morning and go to work. But, for somebody like Janice, the opportunity and ability to earn a living was a great blessing. She lived to work. Other than her children, work was what she enjoyed above all other activities, and she was good at it. She was so proud to be pulling her own weight in society that she wrote to Tennessee Governor Lamar Alexander to thank him for the Department of Vocational Rehabilitation and the opportunity to pay taxes. Janice wrote,

"There is no way to adequately tell you what working does for me. Every morning I wake up with a feeling of self-worth and anticipation.

Your counselors have helped to give me a new life instead of facing a life of nothingness...Because of Vocational Rehabilitation's wonderful work, I am now a taxpayer...".

Governor Alexander was so impressed with Janice that he wrote her back and later that year named her the Tennessee Outstanding Citizen of the Year.

Because of her Miss Tennessee Wheelchair title

and being named Citizen of the Year, Janice was invited to appear on the Teddy Bart Show in Nashville. This was a very successful, well-respected daily television talk show. She was thrilled to be invited. She told them that she wanted to keep the discussion of the abuse to a minimum, and focus on the accomplishments since then. They agreed.

"So, when did the abuse start?" Teddy Bart asked Janice while filming the show.

Janice was stunned. *They promised me they wouldn't focus on the abuse,* she thought. There was no other choice but to go with it.

"It started about two months after we were married," she answered.

"Did you have any indication of his abusive nature while you were dating?" He prodded some more.

"I did have a few instances that caused me to be concerned, but like all teenage girls, I thought they were just flukes and passed them off. Love is truly blind. Most of the time we see what we want to see in people that we love. It's only afterwards that we realize that there were warning signs all along," Janice graciously answered all his questions. When Teddy Bart finished questioning her about her life before the shootings, he took the conversation in a totally unexpected direction.

"So, tell me Janice, would you ever get married again?" Teddy asked.

"Are you asking?" Janice joked, forgetting that she was being recorded.

The entire studio burst out laughing. No one ever

pulled a joke on Teddy Bart. The cameramen and directors were bent over double. The live band was cracking up. The studio audience was hooping and hollering, and Teddy got down on one knee like he was proposing.

When Janice realized what she had said, and what he was doing, she started turning a shade of red to match her hair.

"Get up!" she said, mortified.

He got up, laughing at her and himself. It was a great show and an experience that Janice would never forget.

In 1982, WBGY radio station started having financial difficulties. Soon afterwards, they had to lay off several employees and Janice was one of them. However, another radio station in Lynchburg hired her and her broadcast career continued. She worked there for several months, but they were forced to close down and once again, she found herself unemployed. The depression of losing the work that she loved was extremely difficult. For a period of time, the job loss took away her self-worth and self-confidence. She stayed home for weeks on end without showing interest in doing anything. Slowly she started to bounce back as Joe, Wilma, Kay, and the children kept her busy with family activities.

Janice settled herself down into a routine lifestyle. She continued to get out and go as often as possible and she enjoyed watching her children enter and exit their teenage years. After all the horror and pain that Janice had experienced, all the dozens of surgeries she had lived through, all the physical therapy that she had endured, God had still provided her a beautiful life. A life full of happiness and laughter, a life full of heartache and pain, a life with people around her that loved her dearly, a life that only God could salvage. All glory to Him!

Wilma, Joe, Kay, and Janice

Jason, Julie, and Joey

Maxine
Janice's lifelong friend

photo provided by Maxine Dean

Pastor Jack Hice
and wife
Joyce

photo provided by Pastor Hice

Kim and Jada

photo provided by Kim and Jada

Kenneth, Kim,
and Jada

photo provided by Kim and Jada

Kay and Wilma
Mother's Day
2006

photo provided by Carol Farris

West End Baptist Church

Where are they now?

Janice

During the 1980s, Janice enjoyed many trips with her family. She was in relatively good health and still got out regularly. While Joey was away at college, the entire family drove to Maryville, Tennessee for a family reunion at Joe's step-sister's house. Janice was thrilled when Joey surprised them by driving the three hours from school to be with the family. The trip was a highlight for Janice. She loved to travel and enjoy herself, and the fact that her family wasn't about to let her disability keep them, or her, from enjoying life, was a very big encouragement. Right after the shootings, the doctors had told her that due to the condition of her body, her life expectancy was about ten years. She was determined to enjoy every bit of life that the Lord blessed her with, and she was equally as determined to prove the doctors wrong.

In 1987, Joe, Wilma, Janice, and Julie took a trip to Asheville, North Carolina. They toured the Biltmore Mansion and then drove the beautiful Blue Ridge Parkway over to Gatlinburg. It was hard to keep Janice at home. Even when she wasn't traveling, she was able to get out of the house several times a week. Every Friday, Janice and Wilma would go to the beauty parlor to have their hair done before the weekend. She also attended church every Sunday. In 1989, Kim, Kay's oldest daughter, had her first child, a beautiful, petite girl named Laken. Since Kim worked full-time, after she finished her six weeks maternity leave, she asked Wilma and Janice if they would keep Laken for her. This was practically a life-saver for Janice. Even though she was still active and going out several times each week, having the baby around broke the monotony of being in the bed all day. Janice would hold her while Wilma was busy working in the house and every day Laken would take her nap with Janice. They took her everywhere they had to go, even to the beauty parlor. In 1990, Jada, Kay's youngest daughter, had her first child, a boy named Austin. Wilma and Janice also kept him occasionally.

The 1990s brought a lot of change in Janice's world. She was excited that she had lived long enough to see her children graduate from high school and college and to see them start their own lives. It was also a milestone for Janice when she witnessed all three of her children give their lives to the Lord. There was nothing more important to her than seeing them love and put their trust in Jesus. She knew what it meant to have Him as Lord, Savior, and best Friend. He had carried her through many valleys of the shadow of death and he had extended her life far beyond the predictions of man. Life was hard, but it would be a million times harder without the loving comfort that she received from the Lord.

Over the next few years, Janice had several grandchildren of her own. Life just kept getting better and better. She still struggled with health issues from time to time and there were always the particular problems that arose for someone that was a quadriplegic, but overall, Janice was enjoying a good life.

However, life took a turn for the worse in 1993 when Joe was diagnosed with Alzheimer's. Janice was devastated. For the next eight years, she watched her daddy change. She could talk to the person who looked like her daddy, but when he responded, it was as though she was talking to a complete stranger. As he progressed through the disease, it was as if she lost her daddy over and over again, yet he was still there. It was painful and agonizing to watch him go down. And that wasn't even half the pain. She was also watching Wilma lose her life-long companion, and, as hard as it was on Janice, it was exponentially harder on Wilma. By the time he got to the point that he no longer knew anyone or even anything about himself, Wilma was in turmoil. *What should she do?* She had a daughter who needed her and a husband that didn't know her anymore. Wilma cried and agonized over the decision, but finally came to the conclusion that Joe would have to be put into a facility. She could no longer help him, but she could still help Janice. In 2001, Joe moved out of the house and into a nursing facility. Wilma drove to see him everyday.

Right after Joe was placed in the facility, Kay became ill. She was diagnosed with COPD, fibromyalgia, and arterial disease. The arterial disease was preventing her legs from receiving proper blood flow, so the surgeons reconstructed her aorta as it split to travel down each leg. The next two years saw Joe and Kay getting worse, and Wilma was about to buckle under the weight of worry.

In February 2003, the nursing facility where Joe lived called the family to come. They informed the family that it wouldn't be long before Joe passed away. The whole family was with him on his last day and the Lord graciously allowed Joe to wake up and recognize everybody. After about an hour of talking to them, he slipped back into a deep sleep. Friends of the family had arrived and they took Wilma out into the hallway to explain to her that she needed to tell him that it was okay to go on. She struggled with the thought, but finally gave in. Right after she lovingly told Joe that it was okay and that he could go on home to heaven, he breathed his last.

The following years were the hardest Janice could ever remember, even harder than the first years after the shootings. It was so difficult to reconcile herself to the fact that Joe would never come walking through her door again, but it was even harder to watch her mama. They had been married for 58 years and Wilma had no desire to go on or to do anything after Joe passed away. She would often say, "I just wish that I would go on too".

For the next four years, they struggled through life, with the help of the children, then Wilma's health started to decline. Kay's health was also still deteriorating, so in 2009, Kay and Kenneth moved in with Wilma and Janice. Wilma had become weaker and had started to fall more often. Janice was afraid that her mama would fall at the other end of the house and she wouldn't know it, so the arrangement was a good one for everyone involved. Not long after they moved in, Wilma was put in a hospital bed with Hospice care. She had stopped eating and drinking and soon had kidney failure. All the fight had gone out of her, and she left to be with her Joe in July 2010.

Soon after Wilma passed away, Kay started experiencing constant and excruciating pain. The doctors determined that her right leg was no longer getting any blood flow. There was no other choice but to amputate. Janice was worried about how she would react when she first saw Kay after the surgery, but Kay was smiling and happy when she rolled into Janice's room after returning home. Janice hadn't even considered that the pain had been so bad that Kay would have gladly lost her leg to stop it. However, the relief from the pain didn't last long and Kay took a turn for the worse. She was in a hospital bed on one end of the house and Janice was on the other. They talked on the phone but rarely got to see each other. Whenever Janice had to get up to go to the doctor, she would make sure that she rolled down the hallway to visit her sister before she returned to her bed. As Kay got worse, Janice took every opportunity to see her. It had been thirteen months since Wilma died, and Kay was nearing the end. Janice was preparing to get up to go see Kay when Kenneth came into the room. He told her that it would be a good idea if she didn't come that day, but just remembered Kay as she was. Later that day, Jada came to Janice's room. "Mama wanted me to bring you a kiss from her" she said. As tears rolled down Janice's face, Jada leaned over her bed and kissed her on the cheek. Janice kissed Jada back on the cheek and said, "Please give her one back from me and tell her I love her". Jada returned to the other end of the house to sit with Kay as she went to join Wilma and Joe. She died in August 2011.

Janice had resigned herself to Joe's death. She was numb when Wilma died, but she was overwhelmed when Kay passed away at just 65 years old. Janice had outlived all of them. *Why, Lord, why?* The pain was almost unbearable. If it hadn't been for her children and grandchildren, she would have given up and gone to join them. Joe, Wilma, and Kay were Janice's heroes. They were there for her and stuck by her at the worst times of her life. She couldn't imagine living without them.

Joey and Julie got busy arranging caregivers for Janice, but it was more difficult than any of them expected. They had several that were great to Janice and cared about her, but since she needed 24-hour care, they had to have a lot of different people on which to rely. It was nearly impossible to find enough people that they could depend on to staff her with care around the clock. Joey and Julie wanted to make sure she had the best care possible and could still remain in her own home, but it soon proved impossible. Janice was able to stay in her home for three more years before the quality of caregivers deteriorated to the point that her well-being was compromised. With the degree of specialized care that she needed, she had no choice but to enter a nursing facility. In July 2014, Janice left Joe and Wilma's home for the last time. Joey and his son moved her into the newest nursing facility in the area. Janice hated to leave her home. She had lived almost 40 years in that room where she had experienced millions of happy memories and at least a billion tears.

What Janice didn't know was that the number of tears shed there wasn't over. Joey stood in the doorway and watched the ambulance leave with Janice . He knew that his mother would never see this place again. For the last 40 years, her life had revolved around this house and, in particular, her room. All the memories of those years flooded his mind and heart: the proms, the graduations, the wedding celebrations, the thousands of visitors and friends, Joe and Wilma. After the ambulance was out of sight, Joey sat on the front porch and cried.

It took Janice over three months to adjust and finally accept her new home. Since moving into the facility, the Lord has been gently ministering healing to Janice. One thing in particular that He has helped her through was forgiving herself. For over forty years, Janice had secretly blamed herself for W.J.'s death. He had told her when they were first married, that if he hadn't married her, he would never have married anyone. She felt if she hadn't married him that he would not have killed himself; therefore, in her mind, it was her fault that he died. Janice finally came to the place where she realized that she did everything that she could for W.J. and that it wasn't her fault. She very rarely even thinks about him anymore, but when she does see him in her memories now, she no longer sees the monster. Instead, she sees the look in his eyes and the smile on his face that she fell in love with. The look that says "I love you". Recently, Janice heard a song by the musical group Little Big Town entitled *A Better Man*. The song expressed what she had wondered for years. What would life have been like if W.J.

had been a better man? She readily admits that she also had room to improve, but oh, the things they could have enjoyed, if he had just changed early in their married life.

The Lord has also delivered her from the nightmares that had occasionally plagued her since the shootings. Janice knows, beyond a shadow of a doubt, that she couldn't have made it without Jesus, and after all the bad things that He has brought her through, she knows that there are only good things to come. Looking back, Janice has diagnosed her naiveté during her younger years as "chronic stupidity". Even now, after all she's endured, she still has her sense of humor.

Janice will always carry the pain of not getting her children out of the situation sooner, but she is grateful that they all lived through it. Her other regret is not writing this book earlier in life. The Lord has relentlessly pursued her about putting her story on paper to help other women who may find themselves in a similar position. Realizing that you can't outrun God, she finally gave in to His urging in June 2016. Janice is glad that she did relent to writing the book because she has found a different kind of peace through the process. It has brought a final peace with the past and has also brought a peaceful feeling to know that she has accomplished what Jesus asked her to do.

Joey

Endure

For what ever reason, the word Endure keeps entering my head when sitting down to write this. From the early age of six years old, I began going on service calls with the man I reluctantly call my father. I learned that I would be enduring many things that a child should not. Enduring and attempting to overcome the fear of knowing what was coming if mistakes were made. As examples, not knowing the difference between a crescent wrench and a pipe wrench, not precisely working the clutch on the truck on a hill, not bringing back the right part from the truck and not correctly using a soldering iron would bring immediate and harsh consequences that, as an adult, I now know was severe child abuse. Enduring the physical and mental abuse was a way of survival-although I am not sure that I was even aware of it at the time. Even harder was the severe physical abuse that I witnessed my mother endure so many times and the helplessness and fear that I felt.

After the events of December 22, 1974, the endurance became more mental than anything. Knowing that my mother would never walk (here on Earth) again, that (in my mind) the whole world was looking at and making fun of me, that I didn't stop him or kill him myself that night, that I was awkwardly shy and self-conscious and that I had zero confidence were all very hard to endure. Along with it came all that goes along with becoming a teen: being more disrespectful that I should, a "Quick" temper, balancing right from wrong, the pressure of not wanting to let anyone down and wanting to earn my own way was a lot for me to work through. Thankfully, I was able to navigate through it, but ONLY through God's grace and by having who I know were Angels here on Earth—Nanny and DaddyJoe. Even trying to describe what they mean to me would do them an injustice. They sacrificed so much, but never saw it that way. Tears of appreciation will always accompany the mention of their names.

As bad as the circumstances were, I will say that learning to endure my early childhood did instill in me a surprisingly strong will and persistent drive. That persistence, along with the fear of failure, has helped me successfully hide the deficiencies that I still feel so strongly today, graduate from college and succeed in business ventures.

I am the thankful father of two children. I was forever of the mindset that they would never endure a failed marriage, but that was not to be. The relationship that I have with my children is not what I had hoped for or dreamed of (for reasons that would not be appropriate to discuss here) and they jury will always be out, but I am hopeful of being considered a good father when all is said and done. I have a wonderful woman in my life and, hopefully, will be granted the chance of being considered a good husband and step father in God's timing. God has blessed me in ways that I don't deserve and I am keenly aware of His unwavering support of my happiness. It is something that I will, hopefully, find one day.

I would be remiss in not saying that, without any disrespect to my brother and sister whom I dearly love and who have unfairly endured and continue to endure a life full of pain caused through no fault of their own along with all others who have been negatively impacted by this tragedy, my mother has endured more physical and mental pain that any one should ever have to endure. Did she make many "what in the world were you thinking" mistakes both before and after December 22, 1974? YES!!! Do I even come close to understanding some of her logic, thought process or decision making then or now? NO!!! That said, she has endured literally hundreds (if not thousands) of surgeries/medical procedures, 42 plus years of being unable to walk or take care of herself, seclusion that is just short of solitary confinement, no real income and (although some question it) the guilt of what happened. I am not trying to justify her actions, but in my opinion, God, DaddyJoe and Nanny would not want any of us to feel anything but compassion for her. Unfortunately, society (in general and myself included) has a way of not seeing it's shortcomings, but quickly pointing out those of others. She has more that paid for her mistakes and I continue to ask God to ease her pain-both mentally and physically and respectfully ask the same of all with knowledge of this tragedy. I am not as well versed in the Bible as others and, for me, that is okay between me and God, but, may I ask, in all circumstances may we all "do unto others as you would have them do unto you".

Respectfully submitted,

Joey

Jason

Ezekiel 18:19-20

¹⁹ "Yet you say, 'Why should not the son suffer for the iniquity of the father?' When the son has done what is just and right, and has been careful to observe all my statutes, he shall surely live· The soul who sins shall die. The son shall not suffer for the iniquity of the father, nor the father suffer for the iniquity of the son. The righteousness of the righteous shall be upon himself, and the wickedness of the wicked shall be upon himself." ASV

After graduating from high school in 1984, I began a frustrating five year journey seeking to discover a purpose in life. Similar to a feather in the wind, I attempted to seek the answer by following various paths, including attending the local community college, then a local trade school, then working in a retail position, all within the first two years. In each instance, I began but never finished what I started. Later, I enrolled in a four-year university and took courses in Business for two semesters, yet left soon after to return to Tullahoma to work in a manufacturing plant for a year. A lack of self-discipline and focus led me to this decision and was the recurring theme of my life to this point. Finally, in 1988, I decided to make a clean break from all I had known and departed for Nashville in search of purpose. That is when my life changed forever.

God knows the hearts and needs of all His own. Undoubtedly, this was the case when Beth came into my life. As a graduate student at Vanderbilt, she brought instant stability and focus for me while providing a safe place for me where I could be myself without fear of judgment. Most importantly, she was blessed with amazing gifts of wisdom, peace, and love that remain God-given. We married in 1991 and recently celebrated our 25th wedding anniversary. Not only has God blessed me with a beautiful wife, he has given us three amazing children to love and cherish daily,

My career path led me to enjoy a twenty year tenure in healthcare administration, including founding my own company and building it into an acquisition target in 2005. However, I did not find my true purpose in life until I decided to go back to college to become a public educator. Since then, I have been fortunate to teach and coach at the high school level and now am serving as a high school assistant principal after obtaining my graduate degree in Educational Leadership.

In my current role, I see my students as a mission field for me to impact through relating with students who are struggling with life. My passion is fueled by my desire to help these teens to not make the same mistakes I have made in life. I candidly use my past experiences while growing up to connect with them and let them know I care enough not to let them go down the same road. I love my job.

I firmly believe everyone is a sum total of their life experiences, and how they respond to them is what makes them who they are. As a youngster, I was told never to talk about "the accident." Accident? What happened was not an accident. It was the result of decisions made by parents that impacted the lives of their children. How much forethought was given to the impact is for the reader to decide. For me, however, it was difficult both then and now to grasp how this could have been allowed to happen. As a parent myself, I do not understand how anyone can idly stand by while children are routinely being mentally and physically abused. The circumstances do not matter if my children are being harmed, I will go to whatever lengths necessary to keep them safe.

So how have I dealt with the past? Simple; for thirty years after "the accident", I didn't. I remembered what I was told and never spoke about it. Never spoke about my anger. Never spoke about a lack of self-esteem and confidence. Never processed my thoughts and questions. Never dealt with depression. Then, one day, I perceived my family's safety and well-being were being threatened by others, and my life briefly unraveled due to rage that could have led to dire consequences. Fortunately, others came to my immediate rescue and led me to seek help for issues unknown. When speaking with a therapist after hearing my story, he illustrated it as, since the age of eight, I had tightly bottled up all of my related anger and rage by not addressing or acknowledging them. Over time, the bottle took in more toxicity and eventually the bottle was shaken and the top exploded similar to a soda. Once the contents were out, they had to be "cleaned" up.

Since then, life still has its challenges, but I feel more at peace than ever before. Are there still unaddressed issues from the past? Yes, and they are likely to remain, but I can live with that. My focus now is on how to be the best husband, father, and mentor I can be. My grandparents have laid the foundation for me and provided the best example of sacrificial love that I now extend to my children. God has richly blessed me with the love of my wife and children, and He will carry me onward and upward.

Jason

Julie

My chapter was five pages long before I completed reading this book. But after reading, I felt strongly that I needed to change my ending. For, you see, so many things were not fully portrayed in this book. None of this is due to the writer, but due to a couple of other things. One is that many of the people involved are no longer alive, so their perspective is told mainly by my mother. We all know that there are typically many sides to a story including the sides portrayed by all involved and the truth that usually lies in the middle. The second thing is that there was so much more abuse to others than what is mentioned in this book. Please know, abuse is not just a physical interaction, but can include mental, emotional, and other types as well.

Now, let me be clear and say that my mother does not deserve being paralyzed for life. I have never thought that and never will. Her mental pain that still lingers within and is projected to those closest to her, has been unbearable at times. However, I also want to convey that many, many loved ones were affected by the actions and lack of actions of my mother and father, and to this day, those effects are felt. Personally, those effects are felt by me and I deal with them regularly.

I also want to be perfectly clear that my grandparents, referred to as Wilma (Nanny) and Joe (Daddy Joe) are complete saints in my eyes. They halted their lives to not only care for their invalid, and many times quite demanding daughter, but also to raise her three children, something I cannot imagine doing myself. While reading this book, at times I wondered how they could allow such things to happen to their daughter. However, I also know from conversations with my grandmother years before her death, in addition to my adult knowledge, that some of the happenings in this book are not portrayed in the manner in which I truly think they occurred. For a person to continue being abused and allow her children to be abused as my mother did, there is a lack of mental clarity and some delusion that obviously occurs.

Being a mother who deeply loves her children, I will never understand the actions of my mother and father. (Again, keep in mind there are so many things not discussed in this book.) I will never understand how parents would not die or kill to protect their own. Never. And if no one can understand me for feeling that way, I will not apologize. I have been told by many people that "things were different back then." Maybe they were. What I know is what I live now, and I can tell you that my children would never be exposed to this kind of abuse, chaos, and madness. The things I want to leave with you, the reader, is this: Your childhood is not your fault and you are not responsible for things that people did to you, or you were exposed to, or forced to deal with. Period. You are also not a victim. That's right, you are not a victim. You own your life and your future, and this I say with love and compassion. No matter who they are or what they did, you owe your abusers nothing except forgiveness. Forgiveness does not excuse or pardon their actions or lack of actions; instead, forgiveness sets YOU free. You must be willing to extend that forgiveness even if your abusers never take responsibility or apologize for the actions that affected your life. I know personally that these things are hard to accept. You must also know that your childhood helped shape and mold you. Go ahead and own that. But your childhood and past does not define you. You can rise above things placed on you that were out of your control. And do not let anyone, ANYONE at all, tell you differently. I also want to tell you that happiness is possible through the pain and trauma. Now, I do not want to fool you: finding happiness isn't always easy, but it is possible. Lastly, I want to leave you with the following truths: God loves you and truly wants you to find peace and joy. There has been a lot of confusion in my life, but above all, I know, without a shadow of a doubt that God does not enjoy seeing our pain and does not lavish hardships upon us. I know God feels our every burden. I cling to the knowledge that even though sad and unspeakable things are going to happen in this life, there is an eternity awaiting with our God that is pleasantly wonderful beyond our imagination.

"For I know the plans I have for you," declares the Lord, "plans to prosper you and not to harm you, plans to give you a hope and a future." Jeremiah 29:11 NIV

He heals the broken hearted and binds up their wounds. Psalm 147:3 NIV

Julie

Epilogue

"Trust in the Lord with all thine heart; and lean not unto thine own understanding. In all thy ways acknowledge him, and he shall direct thy paths."
Proverbs 3:5-6

The Lord has been pursuing me for decades to tell my story. After I moved to the long term care facility, He became more insistent. It turned into a daily battle. At first I refused. I knew that to tell my story would be to re-live every incident, to feel every pain, every blow, and every disappointment again. I wrestled with him for a whole year. Then in the middle of a long night of telling Him no, I finally gave in. "Okay, Lord, I'll do it, but you know I can't write or type. You're going to have to send someone to help me," I said in final surrender. Then, as clear as a neon sign, I saw Sheila's name in my mind. After telling my children what the Lord was asking me to do, I called her.

I knew all along that it would be hard to tell my life story, but I had no idea that it would be the absolute hardest thing that the Lord has ever asked me to do. I pray fervently that He never asks me to do anything this difficult again. During the eleven months that the book was being written, many times I couldn't sleep or eat, and most of the time I felt physically ill. I'm very thankful that the book is now finished.

As Sheila stated in a previous chapter, my mama, daddy, and sister are my heroes. I don't know what would have happened to me and my children without them. After the shootings, people would often ask my daddy, 'Why didn't you kill him?' I hope no one blames my daddy for not killing W.J. It just wasn't his nature to handle things that way. There have been many times that I have seen my daddy and Kenneth down on their knees on either side of W.J. praying that the Lord would change him. However, you have to be willing to let the Lord change you, and W.J. was not willing.

There was a point during the first few years after the shootings that I began to be thankful that the Lord had not healed me to the point that I could walk again. I know that sounds strange, but if I had been completely healed, then my parents would not have raised my children. There's no doubt in my mind that they did a much better job than I ever could have.

God gave me three of the most precious children a mother could ever want: Joey, Jason, and Julie. I'm very proud of how my children have grown into successful adults, and how they've accomplished so much in their lives. But I'm most proud of the fact that they've all given their lives to Jesus. Unfortunately, as a mom, I failed them. Until the day I die, I will carry the guilt, shame, pain, and regret for not getting them out of the abusive situation earlier. I will also forever regret letting W.J. scare me into staying by threatening to kill my family.

To my children I would like to say: I loved you from the moment I knew I was carrying you under my heart. And when I saw you for the first time, the love and joy that poured out of my heart has never, and will never, change. I'm so proud of each of you and so proud to call you my children.

I couldn't write this chapter without thanking my best friend, and angel sent from the Lord, Maxine. We have been friends for over sixty years and she has helped me through many difficult times.

I would also like to speak directly to anyone reading this that might be in a relationship. Please drop to your knees and pray to the Lord asking Him if this is the right person for you. Then, listen for His answer. If I had been more mature, I would have understood Jeremiah 29:11, "For I know the plans I have for you, declares the Lord, plans to prosper you and not to harm you, plans to give you a hope and a future." If I had been more mature, I would have asked the Lord and He would have given me a resounding 'NO, he is not the one!' Without the love of my heavenly Father, my Lord and Savior, my children, my parents, and my sister, I wouldn't have wanted to survive that night. But, I'm grateful that I did because I have been blessed to see my children grow up and blessed to have lived long enough to see my seven beautiful grandchildren all come to follow Jesus.

There is a God and a precious Savior in heaven. All you have to do is call on Him in faith. If I had not already given my heart to the Lord in salvation before the night of the shootings, and if either of the bullets that the doctors said should have killed me had actually taken my life, I would be spending eternity in hell. You don't have time to put off the decision to turn your life over to Jesus. You don't know what is going to happen from one second to another. Call on Jesus now for salvation.

If you are reading this and you already know Jesus as your Savior, then I would like to encourage you that no matter how hard things seem to be, cling to your faith and God will bring you out.

It is my prayer that something wonderful and glorious will come from the mess of my life. I pray that the Lord will take my mess and make it His message to everyone that reads my story.

Janice

"Keep the Faith"

One night many years ago
My life was torn apart
I knew my God was with me
I could feel Him in my heart

Paralyzed, hurt and confused
I laid in intensive care
I turned my eyes toward heaven
And cried to God in prayer

I felt His strong hand on my shoulder
And heard His sweet voice say
"Child you will walk again"
I shall never forget that day

There have been mountains to climb
But I know my God does care
It's written in His holy word
Keep the faith and I'll be there

A lot of time has come and gone
But how could I have guessed
With the love and support of family and friends
I would be so greatly blessed

God has spared my life so many times
And I really can't say why
It's not my place to question
But to worship my Lord and God on high

Janice Hampton Quick
May 25, 1997

From the Author

I was there that night. We all grew up in the same church and I'm just two years older than Joey. The night of the Christmas program, I, along with all the other children in the play, including the sixteen-year-old that would one day become my husband, was in a Sunday School room preparing for the production. The room we were in just happened to be the room at the end of the Sunday School wing where Wilma parked their car. Even though we were less than 15 feet away from where the shootings took place, we never knew it. This was one time that being loud and rowdy kids was a good thing. Thank God we were so busy goofing around that night that we were spared the sounds of shots being fired that would no doubt have plagued us to this day.

The trauma of that night, even on the people that weren't directly involved, is unbelievable. My mother's memory of seeing W.J. being loaded into the ambulance after the shooting was difficult. It was a picture that would not be easy to erase. My daddy had been talking to Kenneth on the front porch and was one of the first men to the car. He saw the devastation that W.J. had left behind and went immediately to get Joe. My mother-in-law was the lady that Jason kicked upon entering the church. My husband and I have very few memories of it. I remember being in the room with all the other kids, vaguely remember the prayer meeting, and then walking into the hospital after we left the church. However, I do have vivid memories of the shock and horror that fell on everyone at the church as we realized that this man whom we loved and respected could do such a thing. We all loved him. We all respected him. But none of us really knew him.

Three years after the shootings, when I got my driver's license, I would often go visit Janice. We would sit and talk about everything, but never 'the night'. I found her to be a good sounding board for teenage drama, never realizing all the drama that she had lived through herself. All I knew at that point was that W.J. had beaten Janice and Joey on occasion. It wasn't until I started the book that I realized how extensive it was. They just never talked about it.

I had asked her as a teenager if she would let me write her story as a book. She just laughed at the idea that her life would make a good book. After I went away to college, I didn't visit Janice as much. You know how time gets away from you. It gets worse after you get married and start a life of your own. Occasionally, I would stop by and visit. She was always upbeat and seemingly happy. It was a wonder to me that she wasn't bitter and resentful. I knew that the only way to forgive like that was through Jesus, but she is the first person that I watched live out that kind of forgiveness of someone who had totally altered their existence.

After Joey, Jason, and Julie grew up, went off to college, and got married, we didn't see each other as much. We stayed in church together for a while longer, but everyone eventually moved to different churches. I would see Julie and Joey around town and stop to talk, but Jason moved out-of-state and I never saw him. However, the Lord has a way of reviving old friendships. My husband and I are in the construction industry and started doing work for Julie and also Joey. Even though time and life had separated us, we had always been friends and I've noticed it seems that friends in the Lord can pick up right where they left off and go from there. The years seem to melt away as you get reacquainted.

During the last three years as I've worked for Julie, we've talked a lot and I began to realize just how devastating the choices of other people can be on ones life. She was struggling greatly with the past. Not necessarily with what W.J. had done, but mostly Janice's part in remaining in the marriage after he started abusing Joey and Jason. After Julie became a mother, she couldn't fathom letting a man continually abuse her children. We've talked about Janice's immaturity and insecurity when she first married, her unrelenting desire to make her marriage work, and her naiveté thinking that W.J. would change. Through these discussions, I began to see that these are all the signs of an abused woman. Right, wrong or indifferent, these are the things that every abused woman does or thinks. However, the majority of all abused women are codependent. They can't function without someone else in charge. But Janice isn't codependent, at least not in the obvious ways. She's different. The driving force that kept her in the abuse was the desire to have a successful marriage and family. Was this the right thing to do? Obviously not. Would Janice have ended this charade of hope if she had known how it would end? Most assuredly, yes. She thought that, even in the abuse, she was protecting her children as much as humanly possible. But she never realized at the time what damage would be done to all three children emotionally. She didn't know they would one day feel unprotected and unloved by her during their childhood years because of her reluctance to leave. Thank God she did leave eventually, but not before much damage was done to her and ultimately to the children. The stories in this book are only a small representation of the traumatic nightmare that this whole family lived through. Even if I knew all the painful events, I could not put them into words. There are no words to describe this kind of pain and anguish. They've all had difficulty expressing to me just how it all felt to them. And that's okay. Some things can only be dealt with between you and the Lord. Jesus is the only one that could possibly understand and help.

Despite their rocky starts in life, Joey, Jason, and Julie are all very successful in their careers and all have families of their own. They have been very careful to make sure their children know that they love them, and they have strived to create good home environments for them. They are all very protective of anyone they love. Even though their childhood was marred with abuse, they have all three risen above the circumstances to make sure they don't repeat the cycle. Individually, they still have many hurts and questions. But overall, they are good citizens, parents, and providers. I believe that the Lord honored Janice's prayers for her children during the first few years after the shooting.

Janice now lives in a long-term care facility. With Wilma and Joe gone, there was no one that was able to devote the time needed for around the clock care. She likes it there. Janice seems to find happiness and peace wherever she is. For someone that was given the prognosis of living ten years, at the most, to live forty-two plus years is a miracle. She would never have made it this far if she hadn't forgiven W.J. immediately after the accident. Bitterness and resentment are a death sentence all by themselves.

During the process of writing her story, I've had my heart crushed at the pain that was still evident in the family, I've had my own faith stretched to understand how these things could have continued, and I've rekindled childhood friendships on a deeper level with Janice and her family. One thing that the Lord has brought home to me through this adventure is the fact that all our decisions are important. We never know which choice will affect the rest of our lives. For that very reason, no major life decision should be made without careful prayer and consideration. Only God knows which path is the right path for us and we can only choose correctly as we trust and follow Him.

I pray that you have been blessed by reading Janice's story. I pray that you have been challenged to seek God on every major decision. I pray that you will rally around women that are in the same situation as Janice and tell them there is hope.

Only Believe,

Sheila

Suicide Tape by W.J. Quick

The following is a <u>word for word</u> transcription of W.J. Quick's suicide tape. He taped this before the divorce was final and, as you will see, he never took full responsibility for his actions toward Janice or his children. It is a very common occurrence for people who struggle with violence, rage, or anger to rationalize their problems by blaming other people. It is common, but so unfortunate. You will also notice passages that I marked 'slurred words'. In listening to this, it is obvious that W.J. had been drinking or taking some type of medication or drug. There are a lot of pauses in his speaking and there are many repeated words.

"I would like for this to be my last will and testimony and I would like for it to be known that Janice has said it is her fault as well as mine for this to have happened like it has and I regret it very much. I'd like for it to be known that since this has happened, I have done everything that I possibly know to do to try to reconcile our marriage and to give Janice every opportunity to consider really what the future may be, with or without us being together. However, I've really, know and believe that for sure her mother and her sister has intervened greatly and has agitated and caused this thing to build up to our problems, they were part of it. And I do know, for sure, that the conditions that led up to this was, was not just one of our faults, but the combination of all. And I know that the children, the children will suffer most in these times of tragedy, but no one that hasn't been through something like this cannot even imagine the feelings a person have, it's worse than any death that, I imagine, could ever be. It's something that maybe could be said as a living death that the person carries the pain and the stress through all the time that something like this has happened and continues into his life. I'm grateful for people that have come and showed their concern and sympathy of a condition like this. Out of the people of the church, I suppose that there's not been but two or three at the most that shown concern to me or have visited. And of all the people that I could say that Norman Damron would be the one that has stood out in my mind as a real true man for God. And I'm so grateful for his visits and his concern, and impartial concern, at that. He wasn't taking sides but knowing the hardships that all are going through in something like this. I can never forget the testimony and the concern that Mrs. Mills expressed at church when I went to altar. And I know that there are a number of people that have experienced these things and have somehow maybe lived through them a lot better than we have so far. But I cannot make an excuse for myself that I haven't had the opportunity prior to this to do a better job than what I have. But a person can only know that we were working under such a stress and strain and that we were under and running a business and we were working, we worked ourselves into a trap, into a rut, that we were not able to break. Working six days a week, myself as much as twelve, fourteen, sixteen hours a day. Janice with the responsibility of the children and the home and helping in this, I know that was too much on her as an individual. But since this has happened, I have offered to, I have offered to let her stay at home and not be part of the business at all, to raise the children and to live in separation for three to six months, in order for our lives to adjust to what that she really may want. But she has rejected me in so many ways of not accepting my proposal to meet, talk, any place, any time, anywhere, with anybody, to help try to work out our problems and differences. But, on the other hand, I do understand she could have fear and great deal of fear out of what has happened to her during our fight that night. But what lead up to this is not at all my, all my fault at all, it was something that was a combination of hers and mine and the condition in which we were living. But that very evening I would like to recall that that day she called me and said to come home and talked about our problems. Well, I had no idea that it was that serious with her and I told her that I was extremely busy and I couldn't possibly come home unless, if it could wait and we would talk about it that night. I got home at 7:30 that evening, Joey and I did, and she was pulling out of the driveway. Well, as she was pulling out of the driveway, she asked if we had supper, and I told her no we hadn't, and she said she was getting a hamburger, and I said get a pizza for myself. So, in a few minutes she returned and blew the car horn, and so I went out to pick up our food and I asked her, what was, what was so urgent that she needed to talk about today. And at that time she was on her way to chaperone a Sub Deb dance. The best that I can recall she said that that she didn't love me anymore, or something to that effect, and I asked her, demanded her, to get out of that car and come in the house, that we had to talk about this. When we got into the kitchen I knew that we weren't going to be able to talk within reason of this and one word passed to the next and the first thing I knew I'd I hit her and it then it lead to more blows. Realizing that I had done made such a mistake then, I turned to, I turned to the closet and reached for the shot shotgun that, uh, that I received for, for Christmas and had never been fired. Not taking or having time to (slurred words) go was one of probably the excuses that I can give for that. I loaded it with two shells and told her that I was going to kill her and kill myself. Not not (slurred words) really, really meaning, and hoping that I could frighten her to stopping and thinking of how far along and how serious this was. And hoped that we could reason it out and try to save our marriage for the best of, for the kids and for ourselves. But I guess this is not much else can be said about that except that I know for sure then that I couldn't have done it, but now that things have gone so far that I don't know what the end results could be. I know that for me to kill myself that it would hurt the children and hurt my mother and daddy and family deeply. Had it not be for that, I'm just, just sure and satisfied that this would have done, but how much more or what extent that a person can take, can do. I talked to Dr. Williams and to my my mother and daddy about problems, but I know that anybody with problems, maybe, like that I have, but they offered to help me as much as they possibly could, but they could not help with me, maybe with problems of this, this nature. They offered to do everything that possibly could be done. I know that this is wrong, but I have tried to find every avenue of escape and solution to the problem, but it has become more than I can feel like I can live with. I know that one of the persons in my life that has meant so much to me and is so dependable and so understanding has been Mrs. Ray. And for that, I would like to say that there will be rewards for her I'm sure, but if there be something in this business that she would want, a refrigerator or range or something of that nature, I wish that she would have it with my blessings. My mother and daddy has, has, has offered so much help to me in many ways, but their hands are tied with what that they can do for me. I know that somehow if it had been left up to Janice alone without interferences from the outside, that this could have been worked out. I feel like that it could have. I don't blame her entirely for this circumstances, this is happening. Ah, hope that she will be able to raise the children with understanding and love. I just told them a few minutes ago to plead with her, to extend and reconsider this divorce action, to put it into a separation instead of a divorce. To be sure that this is the right thing to do in order that we might have time to make the right decisions and maybe even to learn to live with them, apart or together. I know that time is running out for me, that I have no other, no other alternative. It would be my wish that Mrs. McMillian, the man in Normandy, would have her washer at one way or two at no cost to us because they've been such a good people to me and understanding and loyal. So many things is left undone."

Other books by Sheila Robertson

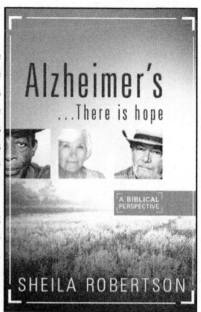

Alzheimer's disease is among the leading causes of death in the United States. Although scientists have identified how the disease works to disable its victims, it is still a mystery why these changes occur in the brain and why the disease is increasing at such alarming rates.

Medical science doesn't yet have the answers to these questions, so author Sheila Robertson turned to the Bible for guidance. In *Alzheimer's* she uses her research to explain:

*Who is at risk for Alzheimer's disease
*The three major symptoms of the disease
*A biblical perspective on Alzheimer's symptoms
*How you can find healing and hope

Today more than ever, we need the wisdom of the mature saints of God, but Satan is robbing the church of its impact by clouding their minds with Alzheimer's. It is time to take up arms in this spiritual battle on behalf of those members of the body of Christ who need deliverance and healing.

SHEILA ROBERTSON has been a Christian for forty-one years and is currently in charge of the deliverance and prayer ministry at her home church. The Lord uses Sheila to minister the gift of healing and deliverance in her community. For eight and one-half years she owned and operated Heaven and Earth Christian Bookstore in Tullahoma, TN.

Available on Amazon

Fairhaven Forest Series

The Adventure Begins

Lost in the woods after dark, kittens Fuzz and Spatz don't know which way to turn to get back to their big white house. Many of the animals that live in the woods try to give them directions, but the kittens don't listen very well.

Cold, hungry, and scared they wait out the long dark night. Soon they realize that they would already be home if they had just listened to the older and wiser animals.

Come join Fuzz and Spatz as they learn a valuable lesson about obedience and listening on their first big adventure.

Author Sheila Robertson loves to write stories based on the real life adventure of her pets and their woodland friends. She lives with her husband in Fairhaven Forest, located in Southern Tennessee.

Available on Amazon

Fairhaven Forest

Monster

Fuzz and Spatz let their imaginations run away with them when they see evidence of something living under the backyard deck. Their human pets don't seem concerned that all their orange things are disappearing, but the two small kittens are very worried.

Will the orange thing eating monster find them all the way around on the front porch?

Come join Fuzz and Spatz as they learn a valuable lesson about fear and run away imaginations.

Available on Amazon **Not Scary!**

Fairhaven Forest

Sugar Baby

When Fuzz and Spatz find a baby kitten in the woods, they think their dreams have come true. They always wanted a baby sister!

They soon discover that taking care of a baby is a lot more work than they expected. When the mother arrives looking for her lost baby, Fuzz and Spatz get an even bigger surprise!

Join Fuzz and Spatz on their newest adventure while they learn a valuable lesson about responsibility.

Available on Amazon

Fairhaven Forest

The Princesses Get a Surprise

Fuzz and Spatz are very excited when their human pets tell them they are going to get a baby brother or sister. They can hardly wait for the little black car to come back down the driveway with their new sister.

Meanwhile a long way from Fairhaven Forest, Little Bit's brothers and sisters are not very kind to him. They tell him that he's not smart enough or big enough to be 'the pick of the litter'. That's okay with Little Bit. He would rather run and play than try to impress the tall couple that came for a visit. There were six to choose from. Who would be the pick of the litter?

Fuzz and Spatz are in for a big surprise when their human pets return. What is that furry wiggling thing in the back seat of the little black car?

Join Fuzz and Spatz and learn a lesson on treating everyone the same.

Available on Amazon

June Bug & Kat Series

The Lost Shoe

The wood pile rolled out from under a terrified Kat as she desperately tried to maintain her balance. Bug saw what was happening and knew that she was going to get caught. He couldn't let them catch him or they were all doomed.

Best friends June Bug and Kat find themselves deep in a country mystery after discovering a lost shoe at the creek. Follow

these young detectives as they enjoy their first adventure in *June Bug & Kat The Lost Shoe*.

SHEILA ROBERTSON first started writing stories to entertain her younger cousins while spending time at their grandparents in the country. Her childlike imagination and love of writing has produced the new series June Bug & Kat and a picture book series entitled Fairhaven Forest. She and her husband enjoy the slow country life of southern middle Tennessee.

Available on Amazon

Ghostly Campout

June Bug held on with all his might as his hand started to slide off the slimy rope. If Kat didn't get back with help soon, he would find himself at the bottom of a very deep well.

When a ghostly figure appears across the road during the first campout of the summer, June Bug and Kat find themselves in another country mystery. Come join these best friends as they piece together clues to solve their second riddle in *Ghostly Campout.*

Available on Amazon

CPSIA information can be obtained
at www.ICGtesting.com
Printed in the USA
LVOW03s0758140717
541048LV00003BB/3/P